Radical Fashion

Radical Fashion

Edited by Claire Wilcox

V&A Publications

First published by V&A Publications, 2001
Reprinted 2003

V&A Publications
160 Brompton Road
London SW3 1HW

Judith Clark, Susannah Frankel, Amy de la Haye,
Valerie Mendes, Alistair O'Neill, Valerie Steele &
Claire Wilcox assert their moral right to be identified
as the authors of this book

Project management: Geoff Barlow
Book & typeface design: A2-GRAPHICS/SW/HK

Cover credits: photo/Nick Knight; stylist/
Jane How at Streeters; hair/Sam McKnight at Premier;
make-up/Val Garland at Untitled; model/Vivien
Solari at Models 1; nail technician/Marian Newman
for Amalgamated Talent; shot at Big Sky Studios;
scanning/Idea; computer manipulation/Paul
Hetherington at Howard Wakefield; retouching/Metro
Imaging Ltd; samurai coat/Alexander McQueen;
design & typography/A2-GRAPHICS/SW/HK

Printed in Italy by Conti Tipocolor

ISBN: 1 85177 352 5

A catalogue record for this book is available
from the British Library

V&A Publications
160 Brompton Road
London SW3 1HW
www.vam.ac.uk

Contents

Acknowledgements

With heartfelt thanks for the generous advice and invaluable support of all of those involved in the preparation not only of this catalogue but also of the exhibition Radical Fashion.

To contributors Judith Clark, Susannah Frankel, Amy de la Haye, Valerie Mendes, Alistair O'Neill and Valerie Steele; consultants and advisors Christopher Breward, Caroline Evans, Jo Ann Furniss, Pamela Golbin, Lydia Kamitzis, Barbara Kennington, Colin McDowell, Jeff Orenstein and Delphine Pinasa.

To numerous people from the fashion industry, in particular: Piera Berardi, Marilu Benini, Murray Blewett, Maia Guarnaccia, Farida Khelfa, Jonny Lichtenstein, Annika McVeigh, Fabien Mage, Julien Mayer, Sarah Mower, Jelka Music, Kimi Nagoshi, Nathalie Ours, Patrick Scallon, Irène Silvagni, Kim Stringer, Amie Witton and Stephen Wong. To the equally numerous photographers, photo agencies and researchers: Ann Deniau, Andreas Gursky, Charlotte Knight, Nick Knight, Inez van Lamsweerde & Vinoodh Matadin, Niall McInerney, Metro Picture, Chris Moore, Pierre Paradis, Anna Philips, Paolo Roversi, David Sims, Marcus Tomlinson, Paul Wetherell and Robert Wyatt.

To my colleagues at the V&A: Andrew Bolton, Nick Brod, Clare Browne, Albertina Cogram, Alice Cooper, Charlotte Cotton, Kellie Daniels, Jackie Desty, Linda Goodwin, Sarah Gray, Paul Greenhalgh, Gillian Henchley, Linda Hillyer, Debra Isaac, Nigel Kirkup, Susan Lambert, Pat McCann, Susan McCormack, Gwyn Miles, Sarah Morris, Susan North, Linda Parry, Jane Pavitt, Lucy Pratt, Sue Ridley, Carolyn Sargentson, Sonnet Stanfill, Rebecca Ward, Oliver Watson and Gareth Williams; at V&A Exhibitions: Catherine Byrne, Jane Drew, Linda Lloyd-Jones, Lois Oliver and Paul Stewart; at V&A Publications: Geoff Barlow, Mary Butler and Clare Davis. To Catharina Holmberg, my very special thanks.

To book designers: A2-GRAPHICS/SW/HK: Scott Williams and Henrik Kubel; book editor, Helen Armitage; exhibition designers: Arnaud Déchelle, Steve Simons and Clare Thompson at Event; sound curator David Toop and sound artists Olivier Alary, Björk, Kim Cascone, Christophe Charles, Max Eastley, Yoshihiro Hanno, Ken Ikeda, Akira Rabelais, Ryuichi Sakamoto, Paul Schütze, David Toop and Yurihito Watanabe.

To Nick Knight for cover photography; stylist Jane How at Streeters; hair by Sam McKnight at Premier; make-up by Val Garland at Untitled; nail technician Marian Newman for Amalgamated Talent; model Vivien Solari at Models 1 and Big Sky Studios.

To Julian, Rose and Hattie Stair, Mark Wilcox, Gail Sulkes, Christine Stair and my parents, Syd and Jean Wilcox.

Finally, with thanks to the fashion designers themselves, without whom Radical Fashion would not exist.

Notes on Contributors

Judith Clark is the founder and creator of the Judith Clark Costume Gallery, an experimental venue set up in London in 1998 to exhibit dress. Clark acts as both an independent curator and as a consultant to museums on issues of display. She writes and lectures on early twentieth-century dress and on curating and exhibiting both historical dress and fashion. She has contributed to publications such as *Fashion Theory, Inside Out, Addressing the Century: 100 Years of Art and Fashion* and *Satellites of Fashion.*

Susannah Frankel is fashion editor of the *Independent* newspaper and a regular contributor to *Dazed & Confused* magazine. Between 1996 and 1999 she was fashion editor of the *Guardian*. Frankel studied English at Goldsmiths College, University of London, before starting her career as assistant to the editorial director of Academy Editions, publishers of books on art and architecture. From there she moved to 8os' style magazine *BLITZ*, becoming deputy editor in 1990. Her first book, *Visionaries, Interviews with Fashion Designers* (V&A), is published in October 2001.

Amy de la Haye is a Senior Research Fellow at the London College of Fashion, Consultant Curator for the new Fashion & Style Gallery at Brighton Museum and Creative Consultant to fashion designer Shirin Guild. From 1991 to 1998 she was Curator of Twentieth-century Dress at the V&A, where she curated the exhibitions Streetstyle (1994) and The Cutting Edge: 50 Years of British Fashion (1997). She has published extensively on many aspects of twentieth-century fashion, including *Twentieth-century Fashion* (with Valerie Mendes; Thames & Hudson, 2000), *The Cutting Edge* (with Cathie Dingwall; V&A, 1997), *Surfers, Soulies, Skinheads and Skaters* (V&A, 1995) and *Chanel: The Couturière at Work* (with Shelley Tobin; V&A, 1994).

Alistair O'Neill is a Research Fellow and Lecturer at the London College of Fashion. He is currently writing his first book, to be published by Reaktion, which maps the relationship between fashion and London in the Modern period. Other recent research has focused on Carnaby Street entrepreneur John Stephen and Savile Row tailor Tommy Nutter. He is also an independent curator of the Sho Gallery, London.

Valerie Steele (PhD, Yale University) is Acting Director and Chief Curator at the Museum at the Fashion Institute of Technology, New York, and also editor of *Fashion Theory: The Journal of Dress, Body & Culture*. Her numerous publications include: *Fetish: Fashion, Sex and Power* (1986), *Fifty Years of Fashion: New Look to Now* (1997), *Paris Fashion: A Cultural History* (1998) and *The Corset* (2001).

Claire Wilcox is Curator of the Twentieth-century and Contemporary Dress collections at the V&A. She curated the 1998 Crafts Council exhibition, Satellites of Fashion, in London, which is being toured internationally by The British Council, and lectures regularly. In 1999 she devised the ongoing live event, Fashion in Motion, which features the work of leading contemporary designers in the V&A galleries. In 2000 she curated Wear on the Street, a documentary record of dress worn during the first 24 hours of the new millennium. Her published work includes *Modern Fashion in Detail* (with Valerie Mendes; V&A, 1991; repr. 1998), *A Century of Style: Bags* (Quarto, 1998) and *Bags* (V&A, 1999).

Foreword

Valerie Mendes
Chief Curator, Textiles and Dress, V&A

The V&A's profound commitment to fashion is well known through the collection displayed in the Museum's Dress Gallery as well as the ongoing series of fashion exhibitions. The enormous popularity of these shows reveals the eternal fascination of clothes and the readiness and indeed eagerness of a metropolitan audience to engage with questions posed by fashions of both past and present. Focusing upon the entirely contemporary, Radical Fashion is the latest in the sequence of these exhibitions generated by the V&A's departments of Textiles and Dress, and Research.

The fashion world operates globally on numerous levels with complex components driven in the main by financial imperatives, though crucially this edifice depends upon the vision and inventiveness of the designers. Radical Fashion explores the creative process of eleven selected top designers unveiling the diverse and often provocative results. Motivated by markedly different impulses and with diverse educational and geographic backgrounds, these designers have in common a strength of purpose and desire to challenge convention. Although they frequently break through traditional boundaries, they never lose sight of the requirement to make wearable clothes.

The title *Radical Fashion* was long debated; the adjective radical being used deliberately to convey a duality. Its most familiar sense is 'revolutionary', but somewhat paradoxically it also means 'fundamental' or 'basic'; it is this two-fold interpretation that captures the range and essence of the exhibition.

Exhibition curator Claire Wilcox commissioned this collection of accounts from leading dress historians, curators and journalists to examine the designers and their output as well as certain radical shifts in recent fashion history. Through five perceptive investigations we share the motivating forces, original thought and ingenious work that make these eleven designers such potent innovators and visionaries.

Introduction
'I Try Not to Fear Radical Things'

Claire Wilcox

The history of any museum is as much made up of its exhibitions as by the sum of its permanent collections. These events mark moments in time, and changes in attitudes, for curators collect ideas as well as objects. Fashion marks moments in time with particular resonance, not only because it continually changes but also because it is a discipline charged with the essence of the present, imbued with the history of the past and full of potency for the future. In the words of French critic Roland Barthes: 'Every new fashion is a refusal to inherit, a subversion against the oppression of the preceding fashion.'[1] This refusal to inherit gives fashion great immediacy, for fashion captures the zeitgeist from Dior's New Look of 1947, through Vivienne Westwood and Malcolm McLaren's anarchic T-shirts and bondage trousers of the '70s to the supermodern clothing of the zeros, described by Andrew Bolton as 'a response to the increasingly alienating spaces of contemporary urban life'.[2]

Clothes are shorthand for being human; they are an intimate, skin-close craft form;

whenever people are represented, whether painted, photographed or filmed, their clothes come too. There is, however, a differentiation to be made for, as Nancy Spector writes, 'Clothing may be considered merely a "dwelling" for the body, necessitated by climate and moral imperative. But fashion — as constituted by perpetual transformations in style — is architecture for the skin.'[3] So, for those intrigued by fashion, certain clothes like certain buildings become associated with moments in time; even with time itself. What more appropriate subject for 2001, for many people the true beginning of the new millennium, than to explore expressive fashion through the work of this group of eleven visionary designers. Although of different generations, nationalities and stages in their career, each has in common a radical, uncompromising and highly influential approach to fashion.

Fashion, through the work of notable dress historians and cultural commentators, has become established as a subject for serious consideration in the last few decades. Chameleon-like, its fascination and significance lies in its ability to function on many different levels: to be challenging yet accessible, to be functional yet to change the way we move, to fit on to the body yet reshape it. Moreover, it weaves in among the folds and seams of a practical craft the expressive intentions of the designer

and the spirit of an age. Clothes have the intensity of the personal, and the power and impact of the general. So, for an exclusive, laboriously constructed couture garment such as Azzedine Alaïa's wedding dress for Stephanie Seymour in 1995, which took 1600 hours to make, the experience of the wearer and the vision of the viewer are linked by the carapace of dress. These are clothes that Georgina Howell described in *Vogue* (March 1990) as being worked out 'in terms of touch', but their intimacy goes further than that. The garment becomes the external representation of an inner intentionality in a collusion of fashion designer, wearer and viewer. Professor of English and Film Kaja Silverman expresses this in 'Fragments of a Fashionable Discourse': 'Clothing is a necessary condition of subjectivity… in articulating the body it simultaneously articulates the psyche.'[4]

To the seasoned eye, even different collections in a designer's oeuvre are as marked with their time as if they were literally date-stamped. Yet fashion is not always about abrupt change, particularly in the work of the designers featured in Radical Fashion, whose output is arguably timeless. Such designers have committed their lives to the exploration of their trade, seeking ever more demanding expressions of 'beauty' or refinements of function in an evolution of ideas and themes, sweetened by what Judith Clark refers to in 'Looking

Forward' as 'desire infinitely renewed'. With such designers, time seems immaterial, as if they are beyond trends or even fashion, in its street sense. In Yohji Yamamoto's work, for example, the nature of change and renewal is explored, most clearly seen when his fluid and architectural clothes are set in motion on the catwalk, each subtle metamorphosis is cut traced in time and motion. Recalled, by those privileged enough to see one of his shows, as a series of impressions, material tracings. Like Rei Kawakubo, one of the most revolutionary of designers to arrive in Paris in the early '80s, Yamamoto's work did not share many of the concerns normally associated with fashion. His ideals of beauty were more philosophical and intellectual: 'My most important concern about fashion is still about breaking some code, some tendency, which I do by using fashion.'[5] In his most recent collection (A/W 2001–2) he collaborated with sports label Adidas in a marriage of art and engineering. In the accompanying press release he wrote: 'It's not about approaching high technology itself… It's about approaching a world made of elements opposed to the ones of fashion.' In a different way Issey Miyake has brought the avant-garde to as wide an audience as he can through the mastery of innovative cut, silhouette and fabric. In particular his Pleats Please line is radical in its democracy — his equivalent of the jeans and T-shirt.

His work is a celebration of the 'fun' of dressing expressively, his fashion timeless yet completely modern. His sensibility is not one based on fashion but on enjoyment of life — a philosophical curiosity that has determined his exploration of innovative materials and techniques and the very attitude to wearing clothes. His approach encapsulates the 'radical' in Radical Fashion: 'Sometimes my clothes are radical, probably, sometimes challenging, but I try not to fear radical things.'[6] Miyake's A-POC (A Piece of Cloth) collection, his current concern, takes 'radicalism' to new heights, for, traced out on computer programmed Raschel-knit tubes, blue-prints of garments lie trapped: 'All that stands between the wearer and their clothing is a pair of scissors by which to free them.'[7] Miyake turns deconstruction back to positive construction, the cut into the healing seam.

Over the past thirty years Rei Kawakubo for Comme des Garçons has also indisputably changed the face of fashion (as Amy de la Haye describes in 'Visionary Japanese Fashion'). Kawakubo's work retains an innocence and freshness that belies the dark palette and subversive nature associated with her early collections that made such an indelible impression on the fashion world; this owes much to her complete independence and originality, and an inimitable fusion

of the hand crafted with technology. Kawakubo challenges existing notions of style and appearance — in the early eighties she shocked audiences with her war-painted models. Like Rei Kawakubo herself, they did not seek approval, they demanded respect. Twenty years on, this designer's collections still feel the force of her fiercely intelligent approach to clothes — a kind of anarchic discipline, for as her protégé Junya Watanabe has said, 'Rei has taught me everything about how to create.'[8]

From the position of a spectator, few experiences are more thrilling than Junya Watanabe's catwalk shows with his joyful, colourful, occasionally even luminous clothes. Variously described as unorthodox and avant-garde, such triumph of imagination married to fabric technology makes Watanabe's a playful radicalism: design totally without nostalgia; celebratory and 'futuristic' in that it deals in dreams and spectacle but is always grounded in the threads of realism.

The constant hunger for renewal in fashion is driven not only by a commercial imperative and the consumers' delight in 'newness' but also by a fascination with image and narrative. Many catwalk shows have a fictional theme, located in the theatrical time of the performance, as Alistair O'Neill explores in 'Imagining Fashion'.

Iconoclastic designers such as Vivienne Westwood and Jean Paul Gaultier lock in to an historical narrative that transcends nostalgia, which they subvert, through manipulation of the form and structure of clothing, for example with both designers' exploration of underwear as outerwear. Gaultier's collections illustrate, like theatrical tableaux, his conscious manipulation of the fashion system. His success allows him to maintain his status as a master designer, at ease within the seductive luxuriousness of couture, while the irony and humour in his work, for example in his subversion of masculine and feminine styles and references to street cultures gives his work a razor-sharp edge.

In her press statement for the recent Autumn/Winter 2001–2 show, Vivienne Westwood is quoted as saying 'to be individual is to follow your mind'. Westwood's work is the physical expression of her thought over her hugely influential career. In what seems a total reversal of her original incarnation as fashion provocateur she now explores not only her past but also cultural history; it is no coincidence that one of her recent collections featured a backdrop of vast bookshelves. Her work operates on a virtual couture basis today, and she traces in both cut and fabric a frank eroticism and romantic feminism, epitomised by

her rustling ball gowns and tailored jackets and bustiers. Both work and maker are complex, and her presentation of both men and women is ultimately that of a designer who sees dress as a key to other ways of experiencing the world.

Alexander McQueen uses fashion photography or the architecture of the catwalk to push at boundaries previously untouched by fashion. In his moving and brave collaboration with photographer Nick Knight in *Dazed & Confused* there is 'a joyful celebration of difference'[9] in the feature on clothes for disability. Much of his work explores the violence of desire. In Voss, Spring/Summer 2001, models with bandaged heads prowled a bleak landscape seen through mirrored glass, while model Erin O'Connor tore at a razor-shell encrusted skirt, literally cutting her hands. Yet such powerful image making is undercut by the ferocious skill of his 'surgical tailoring' (as Valerie Steele describes it in 'Style in Revolt').

While fashion may operate in a different arena to art and not have the same explicit intentions, it has the potential to cross the world of functioning craft to explore diverse issues. In Azzedine Alaïa's retrospective exhibition in 1997 at the Groningen Museum, The Netherlands, his classical 'bandelettes' or 'bandaged' dresses surrounded an Egyptian mum-

mified body entombed in a gold coffin. Like mourners their motionless dignity reflected the stillness of death. Although, fittingly, Alaïa has described himself 'as old as the pharaohs',[10] he may not have had this in mind when he created these exquisite dresses for living bodies (for his respect for the contours of the body drives his fashion). Georgina Howell described Alaïa's clothing of the human form for *Vogue*: 'The technique is dazzling, for just as a woman's body is a network of surface tensions, hard here, soft there, so Azzedine Alaïa's clothes are a force field of give and resistance.' However, the metaphor of dress as sorrowful is in many ways appropriate, for the imprint of the wearer on a dress is like a literal memento mori; it leads to thoughts of absence, of death. As Roland Barthes writes: 'It is not possible to conceive a garment without the body ... the empty garment, without head and without limbs ... is death, not the body's neutral absence, but the body decapitated, mutilated.'[11] This concern is one of the challenges for the museum curator, for, as many dress historians, such as Joanne Entwistle and Elizabeth Wilson, have observed, 'encounters with dress divorced from the body are strangely alienating.'[12]

Martin Margiela has continuously explored the nether reaches of fashion, and indeed alienation, from his re-use of old clothing to his series of dresses sown with mould, about which dress historian Caroline Evans writes in 'The Golden Dustbin: A Critical Evaluation of the Work of Martin Margiela'. The work 'chimes with more modern metaphors: metaphors of replication, contagion and simulation that permeate everyday life in the late twentieth century — the computer virus, the cyborg and the decentred subject'.[13] Margiela's current preoccupation is the relation of human scale to the external world, and the distortion of mass and matter (featured in his photo essay). This is seen in work that ranges from the meticulous expansion to human scale of dolls' clothes — 'every detail and disproportion respected' — to his series of jackets constructed to colossal size. In his exploration of micro- and macrocosmic views of order, clothes shrunk or expanded to scale, which somehow both diminish and enhance the wearer, Margiela questions our place within the inherent dimensions and structure of society.

The work of the designers featured in Radical Fashion could perhaps be linked only by its differences, yet there are threads between the generations, between places and times, influences and inspirations. Each engages with the industry in different ways, pushing at the structure and rituals of fashion. Hussein Chalayan remains defiantly independent of commerce; his shows are like living art installations and his work, which includes film, and furniture that transforms into clothes, appeared at London's Tate Modern in 2001 in its first major exhibition, Century City. His Spring/Summer 2001 show featured models acting as automatons as they shattered their alter egos, dresses made of sugar. This was preceded by a computer-generated film, played to the sound of a live orchestra, which moved towards its sinister end as model shot down model, in the dreamlike indifference and land-scapeless world of the computer game.

Chalayan is working currently with Nick Knight on the presentation of a 'virtual' collection. This conceptual aspect of his clothes does not negate the fact that they are simple and wearable. Their minimalism is a result of painstaking research and thought. 'When people talk about clothes,' Chalayan says, 'they don't talk … in the social or cultural context, they just take them at face value. That's not something that interests me.'[14] From his dresses with memory wires that elevate the skirts to his tailored jackets, Chalayan's clothes combine a stark beauty with a fascination for the mechanics of form.

Austrian designer Helmut Lang operates within a powerful international company and is based in New York yet remains distinctly individualistic, personally controlling product and image. When asked what his label represents he replied: 'It says Helmut Lang on it. Everything I know is in it.'[15] His clothing is, at its simplest, defined by a sophisticated inter-pretation of utilitarian wear, and certainly it resembles a uniform for urban living. Yet his uncompromising approach means that his collections are masterpieces balanced on the thin line between decadence and classicism. For those who wear Lang, his clothes are empowering and exude an effortless confidence, as if made for city-dwelling Valkyrie. On that level alone, apart from his experimentation with alternative fabrics, his work has led to an influential and radical shift in the notion of 'modern' dress.

What this group of designers has in common is the confidence to cut through not only fabric but also ideas. This is expressed through their craft, their skilled intercision, from Watanabe's perspex seams slicing through thick, brightly coloured tweed to the energy of Westwood's diagonal folds and Alaïa's encircling zips and his bandeaux whose seams appear to be made of flesh. These dynamic cuts into the realm of cloth, tracing the body form in the flat, operate as if the very fabric of their clothes is woven through with thought. This craft basis of work is achieved while embracing changes in technology, from Lang's modern fabrics to Kawakubo's incorporation of nylon — not as a substitute but for its own qualities. Underlying radical appearances lie craft skills learnt through years of refinement, experimentation and sheer hard work — but craft that embraces technology. This is perhaps best summed up in Alexander McQueen's strange but expressive words: 'Let us not forget the use of my own hands, that of a craftsman with my eyes made of steel, that reflect the technology around me.'[16]

It is not surprising that the Italian Futurists identified fashion as a prophetic social phenomenon, connecting dress to the dynamism and the consequent social changes in their visions of a machine society (issues that Judith Clark discusses further in 'Looking Forward'). As Enrico Crispolti writes: 'Their obsession with disorder and asymmetry, with luminosity and violent colours, with the renewal of visual sensibility, led them ... to conceive a mode of dress that integrated the sensations of movement, in order for their dress to reflect the energy of a new urban society.'[17] The energy of contemporary society is well reflected in the designers in Radical Fashion: their work is optimistic and ultimately liberating for they challenge every preconception and, at the same time, present solutions. Perhaps this is why the *New York Times*

asked in 1996 of Comme des Garçons, 'What does it mean when the world's foremost avant-garde designer presents such an optimistic vision?'[18]

Radical Fashion is not only about an expressive or visionary individualism but also, in the nature of fashion, it is a barometer of a changing world and changing ways of thinking. The fashion phenomenon encompasses shifting patterns of consumerism, ideas of public image and a sense of individualism, enriched by music, film and literature, fine art and philosophy. The preoccupation with rapid change of ideas and image, and the connection of layers of information makes fashion the perfect vehicle for mass consent to an expressive individualism.

A shift in the underlying fabric of society and the arrival of new forms of information technology — the anarchic, democratic 'liquid experience' of the internet — mean that society is moving from a linear, chronological classification of information to a connective, interactive one, something that museums are being forced to acknowledge. In the words of Caroline Evans: 'Modernity puts fashion centre stage as part of the theatricalization of everyday life and the staging of the self ... With the new electronic media comes a profound change in cultural

identity; like Baudelaire's dandy, we endeavour to know ourselves through various visual fictions which are played out in the spectacular arenas of fashion and the newer media.'[19]

The issues of movement, motion and dynamism that the Futurists embraced are central to dress and the core of the challenge to exhibitions of dress. For many fashion designers a static museum exhibition can be a particularly strange notion: why freeze frame, in a book or exhibition, a vibrant, living discipline that is only brought alive by movement and the tactile qualities of cloth and texture? It is not surprising that some should prefer to use images or film. However, radical designers can perhaps educate museums about the possibilities of radical change in our approach to fashion, as both curators and commentators, for we share the same concern that such displays invariably fail to convey the fugitive nature of 'appearances'. In the words of Merce Cunningham (*New York Times*, 7 September 1997): 'You have to fight for it, keep track or it becomes like a museum.'

While Radical Fashion looks at the work of original thinkers and creators as they want to be seen — that is, with their generous collaboration — it also pays tribute to the visual fictions that are fed by the originality of the participating designers. Technology can help us to understand that most transient and immediate quality about fashion: it is composed of change, and a single garment operates much like a film still. Fashion designers rarely work in isolation and in order to express their vision collaborate with graphic and art designers, photographers and stylists, whose input is seen in the visual sections dedicated to each designer in this book. In the presentation of their work they also co-operate with video, sound and light artists, musicians and poets, architects and fine artists, which is reflected in the exhibition. Specific partnerships include collaborations between photographers such as Cindy Sherman and Rei Kawakubo, and Issey Miyake's Pleats Please artist series with Irving Penn. They emerge in Yohji Yamamoto's appearance as the subject of film maker Wim Wender's *Notebook on Cities and Clothes* (1990). They are evident in the unity of purpose of artist Jenny Holzer and Helmut Lang. Holzer's exploration of the cadences of language is echoed in Lang's tracings of routes on fabrics, as if drawing upon the body a survival map of the city.

Fashion in 2001 has a tribute to pay to these living, contemporary designers, who, in their different ways, have changed its face and made an impact on the wider world of art and design. Its very location

globally — on the internet, in shops and magazines — might suggest the loss of a sense of 'place' as cities and countries grow closer through technology. But fashion is still inevitably traditional and craft based, be it located in Japan or London, New York or Paris (as Susannah Frankel illustrates in her piece on the Paris of Alaïa and Gaultier). Moreover, each designer demonstrates by their creative response what being a free radical is really about by pushing boundaries, challenging preconceptions, exceeding limitations and ultimately finding a balance between conformity and eccentricity, function and adornment.

This is fashion in 2001 at its most innovative and visionary, going the full stretch from dream to reality. However, as Vivienne Westwood expresses it, 'As soon as you begin to use a word like "radical" to describe fashion you are faced with a paradox: in order to do anything original you have to build it on tradition.' All fashion has a connection with past and future, but, at its best, any work that is radical carries the hallmark of the truly original.

1   Barthes, *The Fashion System*, p.273.

2   Bolton, *The Supermodern Wardrobe*.

3   Nancy Spector, 'Freudian "Slips": Dressing the Ambiguous Body' in Celant.

4   Kaja Silverman, 'Fragments of Fashionable Discourse' in Benstock and Ferriss, p.183.

5   Interview with Yohji Yamamoto by Susannah Frankel, *Guardian Weekend*, Fashion Special, 28 September 1996, p.4.

6   Interview with Issey Miyake, *Guardian Weekend*, 19 July 1997.

7   Instruction leaflet, A-POC, Issey Miyake S/S 1999 Collection.

8   *i-D*, no.195, March 2000, p.244.

9   *Dazed & Confused*, guest ed. McQueen, September 1998, p.68.

10 Quoted in Mendes, p.113.

11 Barthes, quoted by Spector in Celant, p.103.

12 Joanne Entwistle and Elizabeth Wilson, 'The Body Clothed' in exh. cat., Hayward Gallery, p.110.

13 *Fashion Theory*, 2:1, March 1998, p.73.

14 Interview by Susannah Frankel with Hussein Chalayan, *The Independent Fashion Magazine*, S/S 2000, p.8.

15 *Nova*, no.9, February 2001, p.108.

16 *i-D*, no.183, January — February 1999.

17 'The "Futurist Reconstruction" of Fashion', Celant, p.41.

18 *The New York Times*, 14 March 1996; quoted in Celant, p.339.

19 Caroline Evans, 'Mutability and Modernity: The 1990s' in exh. cat. Hayward Gallery, p.98.

Looking Forward
Historical Futurism

Judith Clark

The tradition of the dead generations weighs like a nightmare on the minds of the living. And, just when they appear to be engaged in the revolutionary transformation of themselves ... in the creation of something that does not yet exist, precisely in such epochs of revolutionary crisis they timidly conjure up the spirits of the past to help them; they borrow their names, slogans and costumes so as to stage the new world-historical scene in this venerable disguise and borrowed language ... In the same way the beginner who has learned a new language always retranslates it into his mother tongue: he can only be said to have appropriated the spirit of the new language and to express himself in it freely when he can manipulate it without reference to the old, and when he forgets his original language while using the new one.

Successful translation usually refers to the degree of faithfulness to a text in all its nuances, not deviation from it. It is therefore interesting that Marx, in his opening to *The Eighteenth Brumarie of Louis Bonaparte*, provides us with the idea of translation as an analogy for revolution, or in this context radicalism. Confusing perhaps is his use of the term 'original', which in creative terms means both that with no precedent, the first, and that which is new. Yet to describe such translation from the privileged vantage-point of fashion is to highlight the need both for change — our re-invention as more daring and successful, beautiful, desirable and fashionable — and for consensus, or legitimisation, and to accept its inherent paradox. The fashion system relies on these definitions for its perpetuation and its biannual consumption.

How do we recognise a design project as radical? How far does it need to deviate from the roots implied in the word itself, and how do we develop a language with which to describe it? As increasingly sophisticated viewers of fashion where have we learnt to look for the tools used by fashion designers at the forefront of the avant-garde? Chalayan's technological muse, Margiela's slogans or the dramatic asymmetry of Alexander McQueen's tailoring: all provide us with new answers to the many-stranded questions that have persisted throughout the century, questions that are contained very explicitly and provocatively in the reading of the Futurist project. Fashion celebrates the new, that which has never been seen before, as proof of progress, genius or inspiration; yet terms such as 'timeless elegance' are frequently used as synonymous with good. This paradox is central when looking at the role that fashion played within the Futurist movement. The Futurists desired a total 'reconstruction of the universe' through their endeavour to identify conditions for perpetual change — and the 'dynamic' tension that resulted from this equation — and, by definition, through prescriptive fixed design.

Futurism's relationship with fashion has been largely omitted from the history of fashion design, considerably overlooked when compared, for example, to fashion's love affair with Surrealism. This is in the most part the consequence of the Surrealists' direct collaborations with Parisian couturiers and Surrealism's love affair with photography, reality's representational double. The images that emerged from this alliance were widely shown in fashion magazines and achieved Surrealism international renown, while, conversely, Futurist dress designs became relegated to a small subset of painting. This unfortunate historical quirk is misleading in its consignment of Futurism to a footnote in fashion. The reality is that the Movement's powerful association with the rhetoric of change has underwritten the immediate communicative power of radical design throughout the twentieth century.

Within the Department of History of Art in Siena, Enrico Crispolti's work is central to what we know internationally about Futurism and its links with fashion, though its publication in Italian may be something of a barrier to its wider accessibility. It is through exhibitions that Crispolti curated and documented, which drew upon Italian collections of Futurist art, and his seminal book *Il Futurismo e La Moda, Balla e gli altri* (Futurism and Fashion, Balla and the others, 1986), that the enormity of the Futurist vision is revealed.

'We will glorify war, the only hygiene of the world.' F.T. Marinetti, Futurist Manifesto, 20 February 1909, *Le Figaro*

The origins of Futurism are precisely located in the first manifesto by the Italian poet Filippo Tommaso Marinetti in *Le Figaro* on 20 February 1909. From this Futurism took its shape, colour and sound over the following two decades as Marinetti found collaborators throughout the arts, from painting, sculpture and music, graphics and architecture, photography and theatre design and of course from fashion.

In his founding manifesto Marinetti called for an all encompassing strategy for renewal, a dressing-up for a new era that would abhor nostalgia (in which he located all feminine weakness). Instead the focus would be on the sensibility of the new machine age in order to make a weapon of dynamic action that would cut across experience in all its linguistic manifestations. A new artistic order was to be established in which the artist would draw inspiration from modern life itself — incessantly and tumultuously transformed by the victories of science — and express newly found values of speed and the machine. Futurism rebelled against the cult of the past that in all its forms, from museums to academia, from tourist guides to antique dealers, was deadening to any artistic endeavour. In the hands of the Futurists words would be translated into propagandistic slogans; statements, through emphasis, exaggeration, repetition, caricature and distortion, would become true declarations or declamations of Futurist intent. Artistic compositions would rupture their traditional frame or proscenium arch, and the clothed body would become a three-dimensional provocative presence within the urban landscape.

'Fashion has always been more or less futurist.' F.T. Marinetti

In the first issue of *L'Italia Futurista* Marinetti looked for echoes of his vision, for sites of inspiration, of what he described as 'divine speed'. He found this not only in the trains, bridges and tunnels of the new and active cities but also in 'the great Parisian fashion houses that due to their fast invention of fashion create the passion for that which is new and loathing for that which has already been seen'. This had to be harnessed for even faster consumption, and his fascination with the fashion system itself, as one of infinitely renewed desire, remained at the centre of the Futurist movement.

Among the meticulous records of Crispolti's book we find a full wardrobe that articulated the Futurist commitment to dress: fabric design, suits, shirts, waistcoats, dresses, bathing suits; accessories, hats, ties (both of which had entire manifestos dedicated to them), handbags, scarves, gloves, even parasols and fans. Each item was re-described: for example in romantic language fans and parasols are the apotheosis of the coy shyness of women, here translated into 'triangular dynamic shapes that could cut across the face'. Their love of ties, again a symbol of formal etiquette and in that way anti-futurist, instead became 'easy accents of colour, triangular — dynamic'.

Futurists enjoyed daring, novelty, originality, even absurdity in its own right, highlighting the obviously associated behavioural dimension of dress.

Dress designed by Henry van de Velde
in Art Nouveau style, 1902

Marcel Duchamp
Nude Descending a Staircase, No. 2
Oil on canvas, 1912

For Futurists both wearer and dress were active. Its visual legacy is predominantly that left by the Italian artist Giacomo Balla in his designs for his Anti-neutral Dress of 1914 (changed from its original title of Manifesto of Men's Clothing in response to the declaration of war). Though his experiments were carried out over an extended period (between 1914 and 1930) they largely conformed to the ideas laid out in this manifesto.

Balla, one of the founders of Futurism and a signatory to the 1910 Futurist Manifesto, was primarily concerned with conveying movement and speed in painterly terms; he achieved this by imitating time-lapse photography. He chose mainly surface decoration and composition as his transformative tool, his illustrative medium the hurried trace of his brush stroke. Balla heads his manifesto with Marinetti's declaration of 1909 'We will glorify war,' locating the most potent creative force within the act of destruction itself.

Abolished were neutral colours, stripes, checks, 'diplomatic' spots, mourning robes (heroic deaths must not be wept over but remembered with red clothes). Abolished also was good taste (can radical dress ever be tasteful?) and colours that harmoniously match and symmetrical tailoring. Futurist clothing had to be aggressive and dynamic (through the use of triangles, spirals, cones, that 'inspire love of danger, speed, hatred of peace and immobility'). It had to be asymmetrical as opposed to classically harmonious (he specifies examples — perhaps a jacket with one sleeve longer than the other or one rounded lapel and the other square). It had to be agile, simple (easy to put on and remove) and hygienic (for war marches). It had to be joyful and hence its colours had to be vivid (here Balla uses the emphasis typical of Futurist manifestos to describe colour 'Reeeeeeeeeeeds, Viiiioooooooleeeets, greeeeeeens') and fluorescent (an early example of its application to textiles used for everyday dress). It had, vitally, to be reactive, achievable with *modificanti* (fabric badges), applied to an outfit both to reflect the wearer's mood and to enhance its impact, using 'war-hungry, decisive' adjectives never before applied to dress. Finally, it had to be disposable, not durable, to ensure fast renewal.

It was not until 29 February 1920 that Vincenzo Fani, known as Volt, published the only specific Manifesto of Women's Fashion. This reflected many of the ideas previously published by Balla. Compositional in intent, there was no real adjustment made to take account of the fact that this was aimed at women, the only clue being the use throughout of the feminine pronoun. The manifesto is divided into three sections: Genius, Daring and Economy. Genius demands that great poets and artists take over the fashion houses; fashion being an art the same as architecture and music: 'Women's dress, if well designed and well worn, has the same value as a fresco by Michelangelo, or a Tiziano Madonna.' Daring is aimed at the wearer: 'Women's fashion will never be extravagant enough' (though for extravagant read flamboyant, otherwise there is a contradiction with the third requirement of economy). Specifically, in agreement with Balla, symmetry should be abolished, prescribing instead zigzag neck lines, sleeves, one longer than the other, shoes of differing colour and shape with heels a different height. 'We shall graft onto feminine silhouettes the most aggressive lines and the most garish colours of our futurist paintings, in a frenzy of spirals and triangles.' It is in this section that Volt coined fantastic and descriptive titles such as machine-gun woman, the antenna-radio-telegraph creature created with various sprung devices to play tricks on coy lovers. Volt pays homage to their mechanical muse. When it comes to Economy, Volt departs from Balla's manifesto most conspicuously. In his reaction to the post-war situation he fights against expensive materials: 'The age of silk must end in dress as that of marble is in architectural constructions ... we will throw the doors open in

the ateliers to cardboard, aluminium ... gas ... fresh plants ... living animals ... Everywoman will be a walking synthesis of the universe.'

'We must multiply by a hundred the dynamic virtues of fashion.' Futurist slogan

If the fashion system was at heart Futurist, then confusingly many of its associated feminine attributes — romantic nostalgia, vanity, artifice and luxury — were not and were therefore to be removed. Marinetti went as far as to publish a manifesto 'Against Feminine Luxuries' attacking what he coined as *toilettite* (toilettitus): a vain and in his opinion morose interest in jewels, silk, velvet, fur and perfume.

The physical and sexual body were treated as almost entirely separate within Futurist writing. The body corporeal was a locus of experimentation that resulted in largely painted formal designs viewed very much within the context of all European modernist art and its cubist representational legacy (bright colours, diagonal intersecting planes and an obsession with depicted motion). The body sensual was at one extreme passive, or coy, and at the other held the clue to sustained erotic promise, and was thereby truly dynamic.

Valentine de Saint-Point, the only female futurist, author of *Manifesto della Donna Futurista* (Manifesto of the Futurist Woman), provided a response to Marinetti's views, which, as outlined in the manifesto of 1909, were unequivocally anti-female. De Saint-Point forced him to clarify his position of hatred for feminine attributes, of what he regarded as the tyranny of love or sentimentality over women's 'animal qualities'. In Paris on 11 January 1913 she published her *Manifesto Futurista della Lussuria* (Futurist Manifesto of Lust) appealing to women to ride their instinct: 'Lust is a carnal search of the unknown ... Lust is a creation ... we need to create from it a work of art ... stripping it of all the veils which deform it ... recognise it as a force.' Ironically, in her theatrical living poems she physically acts out this promise with veils, imbuing the transference from clothing to nudity, from one metaphysical state to another, with the same dynamic tension as that of the asymmetrical, unresolved compositions of Giacomo Balla's painting. Strength and other Futurist qualities she locates precisely in the power of female sexuality.

Marinetti responds playfully with a series of contradictory rhetorical extremes. Fashion's artifice is a problem for Marinetti: 'The naked woman is loyal. A dressed woman will always be a bit false.' In his novel *Gli Amori Futuristi* (Futurist Loves, 1922), he proposes the total abolition of clothes, the 'last trophies of humanity': 'You know that when humanity will be naked, when women will all be naked virgins and married, finally this obsession with lust [here the Italian *lussuriosa* means both lust and luxury], which always results in that fretting to undo the button of a blouse or look up a skirt ... naked we will mate, as naturally as we eat, drink or sleep, without feverish and unnerving complications ... The only ornament allowed virgins will be two lit cigarettes held tightly under their armpits, glowing and smoking next to the red flower of their breasts.'

By 28 April 1935 he thinks again, this time in support of 'new Latin pleasures' for the mind and spirit, 'an integrated dress for a woman to give her body that indispensable *mysterious* charm'. For the body he suggests 'the dress-metaphor which has both tactile and sound components, regulated by the hour, day, season, and temperament to give the sense of dawn, of midday, of spring, summer, winter, autumn, ambition, love etc.' The dress will have the power to be an active metaphor for every situation.

The Futurists were not dress designers but painters, sculptors and poets. Dress to them was only one more active canvas upon which to work rhetorically; they did not want to learn about its construction. Ernesto Thayaht is perhaps the one

Advertising Drawing for
Madeleine Vionnet by Ernesto Thayaht
Gazette du Bon Ton, 1922

DE LA·FUMÉE
ROBE DE MADELEINE VIONNET

N° 1 de la *Gazette du Bon Ton*.   *Année 1922. — Planche 13*

Advertising Drawing for
Madeleine Vionnet by Ernesto Thayaht
Gazette du Bon Ton, 1922

UNE CAPE, DE MADELEINE VIONNET

N° 10 de La Gazette   Année 1922. — Planche 76

exception to this as the only Futurist who worked directly within the fashion system. Thayaht designed the now universally known *tula* (the boiler suit — still called *tula* in Italian) to be worn by both men and women. This was an all occasion garment; only the weight of the material was changed to suit the season. The *tula* was to be monotone and worn without an undershirt. Practical and simple, it was similar in shape and cut to the Constructivists' working uniform, *prozodezhda*, the main difference being that the *tula* was not specifically designed as workwear. Its essential simplicity linked the concept of the *tula* more to Art Nouveau and the Secession. There were strong parallels with the attitudes of artists working within these contexts, for example to Henry van de Velde and Josef Hoffman, to Gustav Klimt and Koloman Moser, for whom the aim was to derive a fixed and rational, even utopian model, as if dress could in some way conform to the demands of modern life.

Thayaht's association with Parisian couturier Madeleine Vionnet reveals a gap in the Futurist vision when it comes to the construction of the garment and to the creative rather than destructive cut of the fabric. It is interesting that Vionnet, whose clothes are described as timeless, elegant, feminine and goddess-like (everything that the Futurists were in theory turning their back on), would choose for her designs to be illustrated by a Futurist. The extended lines of Thayaht's illustrations draw attention to the dynamic drapery of Vionnet's revolutionary construction. The weave of the fabric itself creates the force field for Vionnet; its flexibility when cut on the bias (the futurist diagonal) uses the dynamism inherent to the cloth to facilitate its movement. Vionnet's clothes fell asymmetrically and were literally activated by the body. It is Vionnet perhaps who ultimately legitimised Futurism within a progressive history of fashion design, but the subtlety of her work was a far cry from the Movement's rhetoric of shock and provocation. Shock-weary designers continue today to push the boundary seasonally to new extremes no longer reflecting the impact of change that resulted from war-time conditions but feeding off the vitality of contemporary urban life.

When fashion is presented as spectacle, radicalism is based in the behavioural implications of what is being shown. The extent to which this behaviour deviates from the norm is the measure of the divisiveness that is also its vitality: what would it be like to behave like this? What would it be like to live in a world where this is the norm or acceptable? Where discernible the rules are located in disruption and become our tools for translation: exaggeration, disorder, chaos even. Just by putting 'ism' on the end of 'future' the Futurists found the perfect label, the ultimate byword for looking forward.

Radical Traditionalists
Azzedine Alaïa & Jean Paul Gaultier

Susannah Frankel

Take a stroll down any Parisian street, and there will be no overt sign of the city's fashionable heart. The French are hardly famous for an outrageous dress sense. Rather, an impeccably chic but ultimately conservative wardrobe is the order of the day. However, for all the talk of Milan taking over with Prada and Gucci and, before them, Armani and Versace setting the trends; for all the power of New York's megadesigners and their limitless marketing budgets and for all the hype surrounding our own British fashion capital and its hotbed of young, creative talent; Paris remains the fashion centre of the world. For centuries this city has been responsible for the most radical developments in women's — and indeed men's — dress.

Only in Paris does fashion really make the heart beat faster. Coming at the end of an arduous international month-long season, the French ready-to-wear collections never fail to inspire and even move an audience to tears. And this despite the fact that there are ten or twelve shows back-to-back each day for over a week. No matter that the hapless fashion follower may have to endure freezing half to death in a derelict suburban warehouse to see one of the more fashion-forward names. Or face the prospect of unbearable heat when crammed into the chandeliered ballroom of an opulent hotel to see what one of the great status labels has to offer.

Take, for example, the time John Galliano dragged the fashion fraternity to the Bois de Boulogne for a show where a barely controllable stallion chased by a rapacious Kate Moss in shredded-suede sheath dress took centre stage in an enormous disused barn complete with bales of hay for seats. Or, then there was the season we were given a map as an invitation and asked to travel to designated busy street corners and stand in the rain awaiting a busload of Martin Margiela's models clad in clothes with shoulder-pads sewn roughly on the outside and fabulous fur wigs. Parisians going about their daily work could only look on in disbelief.

There is always the crush and the obnoxious *cravates rouges* — the men in red ties responsible for showing people to their seats. It might seem irritating at the time but few would not admit that it simply adds to the frisson. Il faut souffrir … as they say. And, more often than not, it is worth it. Where else would the exuberant frivolity of Christian Lacroix, say, rub shoulders with the louche minimalism of Ann Demeulemeester? Which other city would embrace the great Japanese triumvirate — Issey Miyake, Yohji Yamamoto and Rei Kawakubo of Comme des Garçons — while still getting to its feet to applaud the svelte silhouette of Sonia Rykiel, queen of knitwear?

On the one hand Paris has Azzedine Alaïa, widely considered one of the world's last true couturiers and a man who, for many years, was that city's best kept secret, his name passed from one sartorially discerning grande dame to another with hushed reverence. On the other there is Jean Paul Gaultier, showman par excellence, a household name, at home and abroad, not just because of his mastery of cloth and passionately anarchic if ultimately humane oeuvre but also because of dressing Madonna and his former life as a television presenter, the cartoonish front man of saucy magazine programme *Eurotrash*. However diverse all these characters appear on the face of it, they have one thing in common: they are, quite simply, the greatest fashion designers in the world, made greater still by an infrastructure comprising the most skilled of craftspeople. They may not all be French by birth — in fact these days only few of them are — but that is not the point. When Paris sees talent, it embraces it, taking to its heart Westwood and Galliano, Margiela

Issey Miyake
Constructible Cloth, 1970
(photo: Kishin Shinoyana)

Comme des Garçons
Autumn/Winter 2000
(photo: Chris Moore)

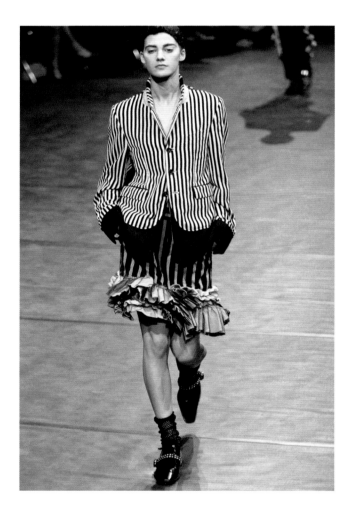

Yohji Yamamoto
Autumn/Winter 1998–99
(photo: Monica Feudi)

and McQueen, Valentino, Karl Lagerfeld and, of course, Yves Saint Laurent. Many of these designers have now gone on to become so much part of the establishment that it would be easy to forget that each, in their own way, has been responsible for pushing fashion forward and challenging our preconceptions of what is and isn't possible in dress.

Azzedine Alaïa, born and brought up in Tunisia, has lived and worked in Paris since the late 1950s and recognises that anyone who shows there, whatever their origins, is eventually absorbed by French culture. 'It has a lot to do with the strong craft culture in Paris,' he says. It is true that the most accomplished lace-makers and embroiderers, the specialists in feathers, fur trim and beads, are all based in and around the city and have been since the reign of Louis XIV, the first king to establish France's supremacy in matters sartorial. 'The French touch is important,' Alaïa continues. 'Even foreign designers who set up in Paris embrace this French style. Even Balenciaga, who was, of course, influenced by his Spanish origin and who makes references to Spanish painters, like Velásquez, in his work. Equally with Schiaparelli who was Italian and influenced by surrealism. But because their work was done in Paris, in French ateliers, with French techniques, it was very French. The same applies to all artists living in Paris.'

To say that Paris — more than any other fashion capital — has jealously guarded its reputation at the forefront of both ready-to-wear and, in particular, haute couture would be an understatement. Even Hitler, who tried to move the entire haute-couture industry to Germany during the Occupation, was no match for French fashion. He would have done well to heed the warning of his contemporary Mussolini who told him in 1930: 'Any power whatsoever is destined to fail before fashion. If fashion says skirts are short, you will not succeed in lengthening them, even with the guillotine.'

The haute couture (literally translated as high sewing) is the jewel in fashion's crown. While Milan, New York and London now hold their own on fashion's ready-to-wear circuit, the haute couture remains exclusively French, and that nation is, quite rightly, proud of this, one of life's greatest and most delightful anachronisms. Shown twice yearly in January and July, barely a season passes without some journalist — and even the odd designer — forecasting 'the death of couture', now only the preserve of some 2000 women. Before the emergence of designer ready-to-wear after the Second World War there were a mighty 40,000 clients. This is not surprising. There are few who can afford or would want to spend tens and sometimes hundreds of thousands of pounds on

an outfit that is fitted to them personally and then hand-sewn and finished by craftspeople who work on it for weeks at a time. The couture remains, however, far too lucrative a loss leader for the French fashion houses, by now global conglomerates, to let it fade away. The imagery conceived at these shows — with television coverage worldwide and daily featured in the international press — gives rise to publicity worth more than its weight in gold. It is no secret that even ready-to-wear designer fashion is there largely to promote money-spinning fragrance and accessory lines produced by the big-name labels. The haute couture evokes more seductive associations still, and with the media machine more omnipresent than ever such associations are far reaching. In a New Delhi broadsheet — sent to me by a friend on holiday in India — one of my haute-couture show reports was, quite bizarrely, the lead news story on the front page only days after it was originally published in the *Guardian*.

The first couturier to come out of Paris was an Englishman: Charles Frederick Worth. Worth left London for Paris in 1846, initially working in the fabric trade, cutting dresses for his wife, Marie, before setting up his own business some twelve years later at 7, rue de la Paix. It was Worth who first hit on the idea of showing his designs to clients — most prominent among

them the Empress Eugénie — on models. It was also Worth who, in 1868, founded the Chambre Syndicale de la Couture Parisienne, a body that, to this day, stipulates the criteria that make a designer a couturier: the amount of trained seam-stresses, or *petites mains*, he or she must employ (they wear little white coats like lab technicians) and the number of designs required to make up a collection. The Chambre Syndicale also fixes show schedules. Worth's motivation in setting up this organisation was purely pragmatic — he did so to protect other couturiers like himself. The sewing machine had recently been invented and, in the face of growing technology, the art of hand-stitching became fiercely guarded in the face of a new, and nowhere near as elitist, order. A craft form that had always been the livelihood of skilled dressmakers and tailors working for individual clients was becoming big business, and a difference had to be established between the two ways of being in order that the more traditional did not become obsolete.

For the designers themselves the haute couture is even now the most precious of commodities. With these collections they are freed of the budgetary constraints of the ready-to-wear and are not expected to follow trends emerging on runways more pedestrian than their own. Instead they are allowed the indulgence of creating one-off garments — most are unique, only two or three versions of a particular model will ever be made — using rare materials and with an attention to detail that would normally be too expensive to produce.

The couture, then, functions as a laboratory of ideas, a place where designers can allow their creativity to be expressed to the full. Such genius will eventually filter through to less expensive clothing, reaching more than the privileged few. Consider Balenciaga's search for what he described as 'the perfect sleeve' — once he found the solution, a strict geometric formula, he took the secret with him to his grave.

For a designer to enjoy the luxury of spending months — and in Balenciaga's case even years — dwelling on such matters is unprecedented. Similarly, if a couturier demands real diamonds as opposed to mere paste, he or she will have them. Two of the most remarkable haute-couture outfits of recent times come from the Chanel atelier. The first was a simple black crepe skirt suit with a single fastening at the waist in the form of a huge camellia crafted in diamonds the size of boiled sweets. The second was a T-shirt that seemed, at first glance, to be nothing but that. On closer inspection it turned out to be made from ropes of the tiniest pearls.

In recent years the haute-couture calendar has been extended and rules relaxed to allow new designers on to the schedule, designers whose role it is to inject new blood into what remains a fragile and archaic medium. In the 1980s, Christian Lacroix was heralded as the bright young thing responsible for making couture desirable again. Gianni Versace, too, was asked to present, adding a touch of show-business glitz and high-octane glamour to the then still rather haughty and elitist mix. Until Versace, the couture norm was to show in the intimate salons that bear the houses' names, with some 200 or so people perched on tiny gilt-edged chairs no more than a few rows deep. The idea was that the monied couture customer could then see the workmanship up close. The late Italian designer didn't let this stop him taking a more ostentatious route. Instead of showing in the Versace Paris showroom, he took over the swimming pool at the Ritz, covering it with an Olympic-size catwalk and filling his front row with A-list celebrities as opposed to the ultra-thin trophy wives of the very rich. Such celebrities may borrow haute-couture garments to wear to the Oscars, say, but the couture customer is rarely famous. Some are known inside fashion for the exclusivity and excellence of their wardrobes — American socialite Nan Kempner is one such. Some travel to Paris

Jean Paul Gaultier
Silk Trouser Suit with Net Hat and Top
Autumn/Winter 2000
(photo: Chris Moore)

with their daughters looking for a wedding dress — this is particularly true of Saudi Arabian clients. Whatever, a couturier will never reveal their client lists without permission, neither will they ever do anything so tasteless as to disclose the price of a garment.

In the mid-1990s it fell to the hands of British designers John Galliano, designing first for Givenchy, then Christian Dior, and Alexander McQueen who took over at Givenchy to draw in the crowds. Up until that time few journalists bothered writing much about the haute couture — there was no way their readers would be able to afford it. The couture collections were more an opportunity to put their feet up, close their notebooks and watch dreamily as the world's most beautiful clothes passed by.

Six months later the haute-couture shows were more high profile and attracted more publicity than their less extravagant ready-to-wear counterparts. Taking Versace's ethos further, Galliano and McQueen put on large-scale productions, shown to huge audiences, where the art direction of the proceedings was as, if not more, important than the beauty of the clothes. While the employment of both designers caused controversy at the time, each proved right the executive brains behind French fashion, making front-page news the world over.

Thanks to Worth and his introduction of a solid infrastructure for the haute couture, Paris holds its position at the forefront of fashion. There has only been one moment in recent fashion history where the future looked less certain, and that was through-out and immediately following the Second World War. At that time and capitalising on the German Occupation of France, Italy, Britain and America had all been working towards establishing their own ready-to-wear industries. These clothes were, however, for the most part, drab and utilitarian: fabric rationing and lack of manpower meant that this was the most sensible, not to mention politically correct way to go. With the War over, the world was ready for something new, something less dour, more celebratory. It got it, in 1947, with Christian Dior's New Look, a style that, with its cinched waist and full skirt, mimicked the opulence of the Belle Epoque and a more optimistic pre-War era.

Overnight women the world over were clamouring for a piece of it, and the same ready-to-wear designers who had previously threatened the French fashion business were forced to provide them with more reasonably priced versions of the haute-couture original. As well as taking over the ready-to-wear industry, the New Look also influenced art, architecture and other areas of design. In his book,

The New Look: The Dior Revolution, Nigel Cawthorne describes the style as 'the foundation of post-war fashion'. It came, of course, from Paris. Today, Christian Dior, still populated by craftspeople who trained under the master himself as well as designers such as Schiaparelli and Chanel, is perhaps the largest and most prestigious fashion house of them all. It is worth noting that both Jean Paul Gaultier and Azzedine Alaïa have been connected with the label. For his part, Gaultier has said that, when, in October 1996, John Galliano inherited Gianfranco Ferre's crown as couturier at Dior, he himself was not offered the post because his role as *Eurotrash* presenter was not seen as serious enough. Alaïa, meanwhile, who worked at Dior for the grand total of five days before the outbreak of the Franco — Algerian War and still remembers his time there with some reverence, was rumoured to have turned the job down.

In retrospect, both designers have probably benefited from this. Both are too idiosyncratic to run with the establishment pack, both have their own distinct handwriting that would be difficult to adapt to the requirements of another house. Alaïa in particular has a highly unconventional way of working. He no longer shows a ready-to-wear collection, although he produces a small one sold only to the most loyal buyers who exhibit it like so many works of art in stores over-run by the less exclusive Italian designers. Even when, throughout the 1980s, Alaïa used to show it was habitual for him not to be ready until after the international press had left Paris. Not that this has ever worried him. Instead, it has added to the mystery that surrounds his exotic name. Neither has Alaïa ever officially produced an haute-couture collection; his name has never appeared on the Chambre Syndicale schedule. Most of his time is taken up making made-to-measure clothes for a small clientele; one that shows immense loyalty in this famously fickle world. According to his following, once a woman has worn Alaïa, anything else simply seems too big. Working first in stretch — previously the preserve of swimwear — and then in woven fabrics and, most remarkably, leather, he has created some of the world's most flattering garments, meticulously crafted to help the women they are created for show off their attributes and mask any imperfections.

Jean Paul Gaultier, meanwhile, perhaps motivated by what he saw at the time as rejection, hung up his *Eurotrash* hat and, the same year Galliano was appointed at Dior, opened a couture house in his own name. He now produces probably the most contemporary couture collection in Paris, instilled with the same irreverent, even iconoclastic spirit of his ready-to-wear

but with an attention to detail that makes it more desirable still. In the past Gaultier has offered up his signature Breton T-shirt in the form of a slender column culminating in a hem of feathers, dyed to mimic the famous stripe; he has created a signature cable-knit ball gown complete with overblown skirt and has even sent out couture for men. His argument? Why shouldn't the less fair sex be privy to the extraordinary workmanship of his atelier too?

As for the way he has decided to show his collections, M Gaultier has travelled a very different route with that too. While everyone was clamouring to get a look in at the new and improved haute couture to the point, almost, of hysteria, Gaultier took his collection back to the salon, investing it with a refined old-school ambience that seemed already like a breath of fresh fashion air. A designer who, unlike Galliano and McQueen, had trained under Pierre Cardin and his school and was fully immersed in French fashion culture, Gaultier demonstrated a restraint that was, unsurprisingly, lacking where his less experienced, younger counter-parts were concerned. While radical to the core — Gaultier continues to overturn convention with his use of fabric and provoke thought through his preoccupa-tion with breaking down the barriers of gender — the designer has proved

himself a master of the great French design tradition.

The differences between Gaultier and Alaïa are obvious. However, they have in common an anti-establishment streak tempered by a heartfelt respect for tradition and the particular technical genius of haute couture. It is the co-existence of these two — on the face of it — paradoxical characteristics that makes them not only great but also exclusively Parisian in their approach as designers. Their contribution to fashion in the latter part of the twentieth century has been all the more remarkable for it.

Jean Paul Gaultier
Oiseau rare: Dress with Top Embroidered
in Guinea Fowl Feathers, Shell Corset,
Taffeta and Feather Skirt
Couture Autumn/Winter 1999–2000
(photo: Chris Moore)

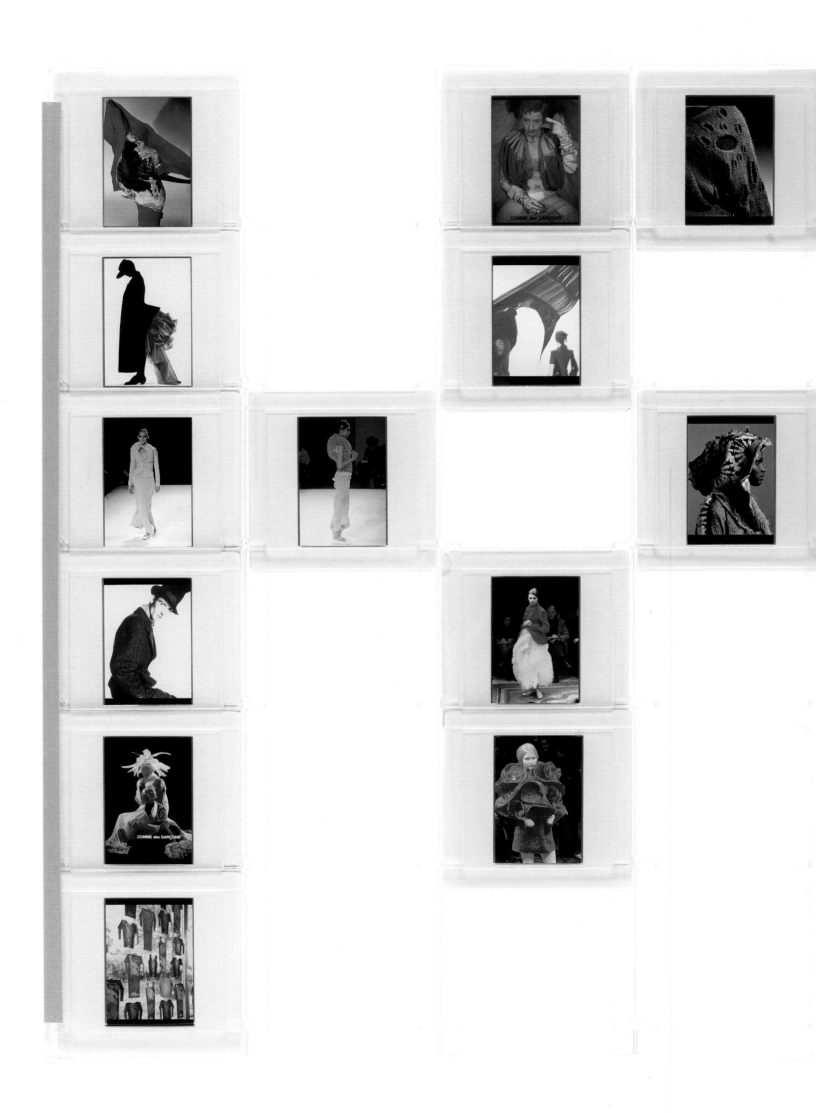

'A Dress is No Longer a Little, Flat Closed Thing'
Issey Miyake, Rei Kawakubo, Yohji Yamamoto & Junya Watanbe

Amy de la Haye

The Comme des Garçons poster from Spring/Summer 1986 shows a black tarmac road, fringed with poppy-strewn grass. This prosaic image has a startling intensity. The highway, open and empty, stretches for miles ahead; perhaps a metaphor for the journey into fashion's uncharted territory. For we are in the domain of the radical Japanese designer.

Described as innovative and challenging, eminently wearable or utterly incomprehensible, works by Issey Miyake, Rei Kawakubo — designer-owner of Comme des Garçons — Yohji Yamamoto and, more recently, Junya Watanbe stand independently on fashion's global stage. Ardent internationalists, these designers are disdainful of any joint categorisation by virtue of their shared ethnicity; indeed they might argue that the notion of 'Japaneseness' is irrelevant in an industry that transcends national boundaries. Yet, in exploring their aesthetic and working practices, there are threads that bind. For example their garments often attract a similar clientele, among them those who are most critical and discerning: their fellow designers and arts professionals.

Since it officially opened to the West in 1868, the assimilation of western tailoring and fashion clothing has formed a dominant image of the representation of modern Japan. To western eyes the decline of traditional Japanese dress has done much to erode occidental fantasies of an oriental 'other'. To the Japanese the rise of transient fashions, otherwise symbolic of emancipation and modernity, have in times of conflict with the West been condemned as insidious capitalist manipulation. It is amid this discord that Miyake, Kawakubo and Yamamoto embarked upon their careers in fashion. As first post-war generation Japanese they grew up within a society that simultaneously embraced western popular culture, while preserving native customs. The tension between these dual identities is explored in fashion collections that reveal hybrid east — west influences.

As specialist fashion courses were not yet established in Japan, Miyake studied graphics at Tokyo's Tama Art University. Dedicated to his chosen medium, prior to graduating, in 1963 he presented his first collection, lyrically entitled Poem of Cloth and Stone. From the outset, and with the modernist's revolutionary zeal, Miyake sought to design dress that was neither elitist nor ephemeral, but simply in tune with contemporary function and style requirements. Often the best way to forge change is from within. After studying at the Ecole de la Chambre Syndicale de la Couture Parisienne, Miyake worked with Guy Laroche and Givenchy. It was the Paris riots of 1968 that reinforced his belief that traditional haute couture was anachronistic. Moving to New York he learnt the rigours of mass production and merchandising with Geoffrey Beene, the American designer celebrated for his high-quality, ready-to-wear lines for women and men, for clothing that was subtly coloured and deceptively simple.

In 1970 Miyake returned to Tokyo to establish The Miyake Design Studio (the catchword was 'freedom'). Utilising traditional Japanese fabrics and techniques, such as farmers' checked cloth and *sashiko* (cotton quilting), while embracing modern materials that included polyester jersey, Miyake's designs were often based on simple square and rectangular shapes. His publication *East Meets West* (1978) details his early work and includes the *sashiko* smock, where it is seen worn by both the elderly feminist Fusae Ichikawa and a much younger fashion model.

Investigating the idea of a second skin and fusing east-west imagery, for Spring/Summer 1970 Miyake designed close-fitting garments with a tattoo print incorporating the faces of rock stars Jimi Hendrix and Janis Joplin who both died that year. This theme was revisited in Autumn/Winter 1989–90 with a printed polyurethane 'tattoo body'. Throughout his career, Miyake has exhibited extensively in museums of fashion, art and design. His Bodyworks tour was hosted by the V&A in 1986. Suspended in space were moulded silicone bustiers — another second-skin solution — and garments of pleated jersey coated with polyurethane. Further exploration of body form — this time a torso rendered in black leather — provided the form for a handbag (*circa* 1990), donated to the V&A.

Miyake, Kawakubo and Yamamoto each established commercially successful businesses in Japan before succumbing to the centripetal pull of Paris. A graduate from Keio University in philosophy, specialising in eastern and western aesthetics, Kawakubo is a self-taught designer unhindered by tradition or convention. Before establishing her label in 1969, she worked in advertising for a textiles company and as a photographic stylist, acquiring valuable skills for future endeavours. From childhood Yamamoto observed and assisted in his mother's dressmaking business. After graduating

in law, also from Keio University, he studied at Tokyo's Bunka College of Fashion, founding his own company in 1971. While continuously pushing forward fashion's frontiers Miyake has generally avoided controversy, but from Spring of 1981 when Yamamoto and Kawakubo first presented in Paris, their designs generated a furore. At this time impeccable grooming, daytime power-dressing and ultrafeminine, fantasy evening wear was in vogue. The contrast could not have been greater.

While western fashion generally echoes the contours of the body and is cut front and back, Yamamoto and Kawakubo wrapped and draped great swathes of fabric around the body. Foregrounding form and texture, in time-honoured tradition they exploited the full-width of their loosely woven and pre-washed fabrics to create oversize garments that moved sensually with and independently of the wearer. (Both expressed interest in the void created between body and cloth.) Even brand new, their clothes had a lived-in appeal, were often multi-purpose, could be worn in a variety of ways and eroded occasion-specific formalities. The duo revelled in calculated disarray, offering garments with disparate weight or length; misplaced collars, sleeves and fastenings; exposed finishing techniques and ripped, knotted and mis-matched fabrics. Their use of colour

was emotive — invariably black. (Equally disarming were the designers' retail environments: just a few items of dress were hung or folded in minimal sites with an industrial aesthetic and hallowed gallery aura.)

Reactions were extreme, reaching a crescendo with Comme des Garçons' Autumn 1983 show. Leading fashion journalist Sally Brampton eloquently described Kawakubo's models (*Observer*, 25 September 1983, p.29): 'Their make-up alienating: only a livid blue bruise marked a mouth or an eye socket, burnt orange and chrome was blistered across cheekbones and eyebrows, and their hair was as kempt as a scarecrows' thatch. Their clothes, too, seemed in tatters — great flapping coats with frayed edges, covered black and grey cocoons of fabric, which were looped and wrapped around their emaciated bodies.'

Bemused and piqued critics issued headlines rife with conflict such as 'The Japanese Invasion' and coined the derisory terms 'Hiroshima chic' and 'Japanese bag lady look'. Ultimately, many were enchanted, sensing that, like Miyake, the genius of Yamamoto and Kawakubo lay in their ability to create radical yet wearable fashions for women of various ages and sizes. The prediction was that their influence would be profound.

(By 1984 the shops were full of sombre colours, rough weaves and asymmetric detailing.) As *Vogue* so rightly pointed out in July 1983, if the European observer felt at odds with the look, the European wearer did not. Among the most receptive to this new fashion aesthetic were the British, already steeped in a cultural predilection for loose and comfortable, textiles-led 'artistic' dress, tempered by the nihilism of punk.

The Comme des Garçons black wool sweater from Autumn/Winter 1982–83, represented in the V&A, is a seminal design from this period. Punctured with seemingly random holes, the hand-knitted garment is a challenge to the flawless perfection of machine knitting. Japanese culture embraces imperfection as a measure of perfection within creativity. The design can also be analysed within an historical context of cutwork textiles and lace; of post-punk expression or even as a continuum from Parisian couturier Elsa Schiaparelli's 1937 'Tear Dress'. Dyed in shades of bruised purples and pinks, the print used by Schiaparelli (based on a painting by Salvador Dali and also in the V&A) depicts strips of torn flesh. Both designers explore a surreal fascination with interior/exterior and juxtapose violence and tatters with elite luxury to shocking effect. Using fashion as their medium, Yamamoto and Kawakubo

consistently explore issues surrounding body shape, sensuality, sexuality and the sartorial gender-binary. Essentially modest and loose, their early 1980s collections, accessorised with utilitarian flat-heeled footwear, were often interpreted as feminist expression. Kawakubo emphasised that she designs for independent women, capable of attracting men with their minds rather than their bodies, and that her controversial cosmetics raised issues surrounding the painted face. Yamamoto describes himself as a natural born feminist, believing his design advantage is that he learnt the world through women's eyes. Asked about his ideal client, he muses (*Guardian*, 28 September 1996, p.4): 'Ever since I can remember, a woman has always existed within me, like a faint shadow. She is not young. She is 40 or 50 years old. She is not Japanese. I don't know why she's not Japanese but she's not. It's very difficult to see her face. She is always looking away from me. I am pursuing her. But I never reach her. If she spoke her voice would be raspy. She is a woman who has given up being a woman. But she is incredibly sexy to me.'

While Kawakubo likes to create unhindered by external stimuli, Yamamoto is expansive in his outlook, blurring notions of history, culture and nation, while acknowledging that fashion is shaped by each. Gradually introducing a softly structured silhouette,

he is a superb and innovative tailor, celebrated for his flattering, often black, suits that subvert convention. It was Yamamoto who suggested the black suit and white T-shirt combination, now the professional uniform for men in the arts. Dismissing neat and tidy as boring he too emphasises imperfection, often inspired by the ill-fitting and dishevelled tailoring finally consigned to Dickensian waifs. For Autumn/Winter 1986–87 Yamamoto showed black dresses embellished with a flourish of red tulle evocative of an 1870s bustle (stunningly photographed in profile by Nick Knight) and subsequently designed many crinoline styles. Other diverse historical references are displayed in long coats, knitted in oversize stitches with medieval austerity; cobweb knits and jet beading with a gothic edge and, quite unexpectedly and much acclaimed, his Spring 1997 collection, in which he paid homage to early post-war couturiers including Chanel.

A black cotton poplin sleeveless dress, emblazoned with an asymmetric flash of orange to form an irregular trailing hemline from 1988–89, exemplifies the designer's ability to create simultaneously the visually simple, yet striking and distinctive. The dress is entirely functional. Worn in the West Indies and subsequently donated to the V&A, the wearer praised both its aesthetic and functional, elongated

slit armholes and floating conical shape that permitted cooling air flow. A seasoned traveller himself, Yamamoto's designs are imbued with international references. He uses kimono silks and oriental prints; was inspired by African nomads (Spring/ Summer 1982); Russian dolls (Autumn/ Winter 1990–91) and for Autumn/Winter 2000–2001 created urban, fairy-tale cloaks with fur-lined hoods inspired by Inuit dress.

Often described as a purist, Yamamoto is also a humorist, who gently mocks the fashion system. For the finale of his March 1998 show, he sent supermodel Jodie Kidd down the catwalk wearing a giant crinoline bridal gown and muslin hat so large four attendants bearing poles were required to support it (see p. 21). The designer said he was playing up to mass-market perceptions that fashion was extravagant and stupid. As well as selecting exceptional beauties, Yamamoto caused a stir when he first employed unconventional, mature and 'ordinary' looking models. Offering a new take on 'bag ladies' and fashion's lucrative accessory, for Spring/Summer 2001 he sited a self-fabric purse on the derrière of fluid evening gowns.

Famous for stating that she designed in many shades of black, in Autumn 1988 Rei Kawakubo announced that 'Red is Black', introducing a more colourful palette. Since then, she has struck a lighter note, sometimes even in tune with prevailing trends. But, more often than not she works at a tangent and remains unpredictable. Possibly her most perplexing output — which left many Comme devotees aghast — was her Lumps collection for Spring/ Summer 1997. Translucent chiffon and pastel gingham dresses featured goose-down padded lumps and coils that exaggerated or entirely deviated from feminine anatomical form. Kawakubo issued the statement, 'body becomes dress becomes body', evocative of Blaise Cendrars poem for fine artist Sonia Delaunay's 'simultaneous contrast' dresses of 1913 (Buckberrough, 1980, p.38):

Anything that is a bump pushes into
*   the depths.*
Stars dig into the sky
Colours undress you through contrast
'On her dress she wears a body'

Kawakubo's contribution to *Visionaire* (no. 20, 1997) juxtaposed images from nature — the protruding eye of a fish and bulbous floral and aquatic forms — with organic looking details from 'lumps'.

More accessible are Kawakubo's Comme des Garçons designs that deconstruct and re-present the vernacular of western tailoring. Questioning the function of the lapel, for Spring/Summer 1994 she used lapel structures to create city-smart halter-neck jackets and in Autumn/Winter 1988–89 for scarves. Mixing fabric weights and silhouettes, her menswear suits have combined cropped trousers with double-breasted sports jackets, featured shawl collars and juxtaposed, inflated and bleached classic checked fabrics.

As part of post-war regeneration, Japan built up its industrial base and now leads in the development of 'techno textiles'. Working with specialist technicians and factories, these designers have been central in harnessing and advancing textiles' technologies to replicate commercially the appearance of labour-intensive fabric techniques and develop new fibres, weaving, dyeing and fabric manipulations. Textile designer Makiko Minagawa has worked with Miyake since the outset, creating beautiful crafted textiles as well as holographic cloth and inflatable plastics for his modernistic designs.

Discovery of a lightweight, easy-care, stretch polyester fabric that could be permanently pleated and accommodate any body movement was the catalyst for Miyake's acclaimed Pleats Please range. Launched in 1993 the designer has realised his ambition to create (Kazuko Sato, p.102): 'An "easy style", like that of the jeans and T-shirt, but one that could be worn in a

Yohji Yamamoto
Black Dress with Red Tulle Bustle
Autumn/Winter 1986–87
(photo: Nick Knight)

Issey Miyake
Detail of A-POC fabric from Making
Things exhibition at the ACE Gallery
New York, Nov. 1999
(photo: Yasuki Yoshinaga)

wider milieu; of apparel that, regardless of age or profession, could possess a modern kind of beauty while still being functional; of a style that would stay trend-free.' Indeed, his egalitarian approach to design has led to numerous commissions for occupational dress, which in turn have fed back into his collections. Miyake's costumes for the Ballet Frankfurt formed the prototypes for Pleats Please, and dancers and acrobats have modelled the range to maximum effect. Injecting renewal within continuity, in 1996 Miyake introduced his Guest Artist series. The designer's multi-layered, pleated silk 'Bouncing dress' from Spring/Summer 1993 has been promised to the V&A as part of Jill Ritblat's ongoing gift.

Some thirty years into his career Miyake continues to explore the relationship between clothing and the human body. This has resulted in his A-POC (A Piece of Cloth) concept, created with Dai Fujiwara, textile engineer and designer at the Miyake Design Studio. An in-house leaflet for Spring/Summer 1999 explains: 'Like a magic carpet, when the roll is unfurled, an entire wardrobe is revealed. Dresses, shirts, socks, underwear, and even bags all lie trapped within lines of demarcation. All that stands between the wearer and their clothing is a pair of scissors by which to free them. The lines of demarcation create a pattern of surface design that

in turn becomes structural seams. The wearer need only select and free her choice.' Created with environmental considerations in mind, A-POC is constructed from Raschel-knit tubes produced by computer-programmed, industrial knitting machines. These garments do not require machine-sewn seams, a development with potentially profound implications for the clothing industry.

To devote his energies fully to A-POC, in 1999 Miyake handed over design of his mainline collection to long-term colleague Naoki Takizawa (he remains general creative director). Like Miyake, Takizawa also challenges prevailing clothing conventions. Eschewing traditional circular hemlines, the Spring/Summer 2001 collection included softly structured, ankle-length dresses with square-shape hemlines achieved by inserting blow-up plastic tubing into the hem. Other garments comprised of layers of ethereal, multi-coloured striped and polka-dotted organza.

Acutely aware of fashion's significance not only as a construct of identity but also in time and space, each of these designers maintains rigorous control over the representation of their work within the broader cultural arena. As well as exhibiting extensively, Miyake has produced and been the subject of lavish publications including the Issey

Miyake Photographs by Irving Penn series. Exceptionally, the photographer was given a free reign: choosing to present Miyake's pleated garments not only on figures but also flat on the floor, as striking exercises in colour and abstraction.

Kawakubo and Yamamoto are fashion's recluses — rarely making public appearances or conducting interviews. In a bid to offer insight into Yamamoto's life and work, in 1990 director Wim Wenders presented his documentary film *Notebook on Cities and Clothes*. During the late 1980s Yamamoto worked with Nick Knight, art director/stylist Marc Ascoli and graphics designer Peter Saville to produce stunning biannual catalogues and has subsequently collaborated with leading photographers Dominique Issermann, Max Vadukul, Paolo Roversi and David Sims to create distinctive, modern marketing materials. Paving the way for the future, since March 2000 Yamamoto's daughter Limi has designed the youthful Y's bis LIMI line, shown in Tokyo.

Between 1988 and 1991 Kawakubo produced *Six* (after intuition, the sixth sense), a biannual magazine of inspirational images — few of clothing (not always her own) and devoid of text. In 1987 she participated in the Fashion Institute of Technology's Three Women show. Along with French designer

Junya Watanabe Comme des Garçons
Autumn/Winter 2000
(photo: Jean François José)

Cindy Sherman
for Comme des Garçons
Spring/Summer 1994

Madeleine Vionnet (whose inter-war work Miyake cites as inspirational) and American sportswear designer Claire McCardell, she was selected for providing a new concept and vision of dress. Creating for a total way of life, rather than an ideal client, Kawakubo has also designed chairs and collaborates closely with her architects; *Rei Kawakubo and Comme des Garçons* authored by design critic Deyan Sudjic (1990) explores her multidisciplinary output.

Describing his product as 'techno couture', Rei Kawakubo's protégé Junya Watanabe is hailed as one of contemporary fashion's greatest visionaries. After studying at Bunka, in 1984 he was apprenticed at Comme des Garçons and three years later was promoted to chief designer of the Tricot knitwear line. Since 1992 Watanabe has worked under his own name as part of Comme des Garçons and has shown in Paris since 1993. Hauntingly beautiful origami folding, honeycomb weaves and garments entirely constructed from or embellished with petal-like ruffles — from chiffon dresses to thick woollen coats and capes — are his forte. Especially note-worthy designs include 'caped' dresses with slit arm holes for Autumn/Winter 1996–97; apron-fronted dresses that could be worn over trousers or skirts for Spring/Summer 1997; garments suspended from coiled wire for Autumn/Winter 1998–99

and an entirely water-proof collection (even fragile ruffled evening gowns) for his Spring/Summer 2000 Function and Practicality collection. Watanabe's 'digital modern lighting for the future' show for Spring/Summer 2001 was chosen to launch the Paris collections. Alongside more commercial striped tailoring, slip dresses and tennis skirts were neon bright colours; tops and dresses constructed from space-age, jellybean discs and rectangles and semi-transparent jackets that glowed in the dark.

It is the ephemeral quality of fashion that evokes its greatest criticism — constantly changing it can be of no lasting value. While operating within the structure of the industry, the output of these designers transcends and is often entirely at odds with seasonal trends. Critics draw on the terminology of fine art and architecture to describe clothes that can defy standard fashion vocabulary. Defined as conceptual — as mind rather than body clothes — it is often implied that ideas take precedence over function. While some parallels clearly exist, the designers are adamant that they are not artists, they are in the business of selling clothes and do so with impressive commercial success. At the dawn of the twenty-first century, Issey Miyake, Comme des Garçons, Yohji Yamamoto and Junya Watanabe present profoundly distinctive collections. In a fashion era dominated by

pastiche and revival styles they are united in their vision and modernity.

A dress is no longer a little, flat closed thing,
But begins in the open sky and mingles with the courses of the stars,
So that she who wears it, carries the world on her back.
The Universe is at Woman's beck and call.

Joseph Delteil for Sonia Delaunay, *The Coming Fashion* (1923)

HELMUT LANG

Imagining Fashion
Helmut Lang & Maison Martin Margiela

Alistair O'Neill

When fashion designers present their ideas, they are never purely concerned with clothing. The settings they choose to frame their designs may well still trade on the luxurious or the exotic, but they now seem to be more concerned with how the image they try to project is inevitably set by what surrounds it. For Spring/Summer 1997 Martin Margiela presented a collection that had at its core a bodice made of coarse linen that mimicked the form of a dressmaker's dummy. Its reappearance in subsequent collections has established the garment as symbolic of the designer's approach to making clothes and to presenting his ideas about the nature of fashion.

The garment implies that the body moves from being the foundation of dress to being its outward and material appearance. Yet this is not our own body, but an ideal one; a system of measure that dresses us all, but is not us at all. Rather like the impossibility of trying to be like the girl in a magazine advertisement, Margiela's bodice points to the mismatch between the ideal and the real, a mismatch that

is central to the dictates of fashion and to its charge. Yet this is not only about the difference between a real body and an ideal body, it is as much about where we find them. Traditionally, the dress-maker's dummy belongs in the atelier, hidden from view as an inert body double that remains uncredited. In transforming it into a garment that is as much an image of fashion as it is an item of fashion, Margiela brings the dummy from behind the scenes to take centre stage, animated on another body as part of the performance of the fashion show.

One would expect the audience to do a double-take at a lifeless dummy moving on a life model, yet perhaps there is a prior acceptance that the women paid to model such clothes are more often than not as lacking in vitality and unreal in their movements as the dummy. In pointing to the artificiality of presenting fashion, Margiela succeeds in making us realise how much of it is fabricated. It is the realisation that for fashion to appear natural, it has to be crafted; that the polished performance for the photographers centre stage is built on rehearsed dramatisation.

The film *Fashions of 1934* is an early example of such choreography. Made in 1930s Hollywood by William Dieterle the film tells the story of a confidence

trickster who conquers the fictitious French fashion house Maison Elegance and deposes reigning Parisian couturier, Oscar Baroque, not by design, but by presentation. One of his tricks involves a splendid staging of an ostrich-feather review with choreography by Busby Berkeley following the salon's presentation of their first show collection. To the invited audience a seven-sided roundabout is illuminated and begins slowly to revolve, each side bearing a historical portrait painting. As a painting turns centre stage, it becomes transparent, outlining a model in similar pose behind, then lifts to reveal her fashionable outfit to the audience. After one revolution, with all seven outfits unveiled, the models descend the circular dais and walk through the salon into the crowd.

The idea of historical dress details in paintings coming to life through the cycle of fashion won the hearts of the audience in the film by its visual animation. As a visual metaphor it is not unlike the relationship between fashion and art. It demonstrates that the cycle of fashion requires that designers often draw from these historical images for ideas. In this instance fashion is framed by its direct quotation from art, yet, like Margiela's dummy, it is only legitimised when it is animated and transformed by the performance.

Busby Berkeley choreographed scene
from William Dieterle's *Fashions of 1934*

Gilbert & George
The Singing Sculpture, 1991
(photo: Jon & Anne Abbot)

The idea of fashion as a performance is currently supported by the elaborate catwalk presentations staged by many a fashion house. The idea that wearing fashion is also a performance is not so readily understood. Artists Gilbert & George have drawn attention to this aspect of dress, to the purpose and role that clothing plays, with their living sculpture shows. While they push at the boundaries of their art they wear their conventional, by now trademark, suits. In *The Singing Sculpture* (1969–71), one of their first gallery events, they wore the suits as they slowly revolved like musical automatons, miming to the music-hall classic 'Underneath the Arches'. Their point was to communicate their ordinariness and their artifice through performance. Their lives are one continual performance, made apparent by the 'responsibility suits' they now wear as a matter of course, which have crafted their identity and become very much part of who they are. None of this is to suggest that the idea of performance is always one removed from life; in many ways the reverse is true.

Susan Sontag has described how watching films gave her tips about style; how, say, it looks good to wear a raincoat even when it isn't raining. The screen heroines she emulated not only informed how she wore her raincoat but also how she might feel when wearing it. In whatever fashion she undoubtedly gave some kind of performance in her raincoat. Equally when art historian Anne Hollander describes in her seminal text, *Seeing through Clothes*, that 'Perhaps photography and film have revived some of the visual awareness between art, theatre and life for the general awareness of clothes' she identifies that moving and still images have grown to inform our understanding of how we see clothes and how we wear them. In claiming this as taking place within art, theatre and life she suggests a frame of reference through which fashion designers work, an improvisation of roles that have been played before.

The attraction of the work of artist Cindy Sherman to fashion designers — most notably in the campaigns she produced for Comme des Garçons for Autumn/Winter 1994–95 — is a good case in point. In Sherman's Untitled Film Stills (1977–80) clothes are used like props, inserted into the composition to provoke a particular response about the woman or femininity pictured. They reveal a tension within dress, setting and identity that creates an image that constructs its own narrative, a story that unfolds beyond the confines of the image. Cultural critic Judith Williamson has written (*Screen*, 1983) of how Sherman's images are not unlike the number of images a woman faces when she surveys the clothes in her wardrobe in the morning: 'Sherman's pictures force upon the viewer that elision of image and identity which women experience all the time; as if sexy black dress made you be a femme fatale, whereas "femme fatale" is, precisely, an image, it needs a viewer to function at all.' The elision of which Williamson writes abbreviates image and identity into a kind of visual shorthand, but in condensing it also strengthens its potential for narrative. This is supported by a recent advertising campaign for Prada photographed by Robert Wyatt and styled by Lucy Ewing that depicts a well-dressed couple in isolated fragments of interaction. The filmic quality to the images suggests that they are informed by knowledge of cinema and the idea that clothing can communicate ideas on screen independent of narrative and characterisation. Here, narrative and character are reduced to frozen, unrelated moments; but in the images gesture, pose and expression are honed to refinement. Such images capture the blossoming of adulthood and the brittle delicacy of desire in a manner equal to Prada's white pleated skirt with its red budding-lip pattern.

After gaining her doctorate in Political Science in 1974, Miuccia Prada spent five years studying as a mime artist before returning to the family leatherware

company. Her background in mime informs her work: her images, the red budding lips, for example, communicate without speaking; without resorting solely to the language of clothes. Miuccia Prada's claim that 'You can't discuss it as empty nonsense. Fashion captures the setting' suggests that the wearing of an image is not only conditioned but informed by its setting, allowing the image to be understood spatially, like a snapshot taken with a wide-angle lens.

This is well demonstrated by a photograph by the artist Andreas Gursky of the interior of the Prada store in Milan. Gursky creates images of our world that unsettle our belief in the structures we inhabit, richly depicting the horror of order. His photograph of a rail of lingerie recalls Judith Williamson's observation about a woman's wardrobe, but here the rail is illuminated and framed as if a stage set before a performance. Here choices, or for that matter images, are displayed as harmoniously as the sequence of colours in a rainbow yet the precision of spacing between each item satisfies each thing as singularly unique. It is the tension between the clinical minimalism of the setting and the intimate apparel displayed that roused Gursky to contemplate on how seduction could reside in such an austere environment.

This tension between restriction and desire is also evident in the work of Helmut Lang

who proposes a different relation between image and setting. Hailing from Vienna, home of the waltz and sugar-coated romanticism Lang creates clothes in contradiction to this aesthetic. His pared, spartan designs possess the utilitarian qualities of street clothes but couched in luxurious, tactile materials, which feminise and soften them. His clothes designs are very much in keeping with the writings of Adolf Loos, the Viennese architect who began the modernist assault on ornamentation. Loos believed the ideal condition of clothing for modern man was as an unreadable surface, a mask of concealment rather than character that would offset a cultivated interior. Helmut Lang's collaboration with American artist Jenny Holzer for the 1996 Venice Biennale took the form of a projected slogan that read I SMELL YOU ON MY CLOTHES implying that interior desires rest on the surface, as if worn on the body. The webpage for Lang's perfume range scrolls down similarly distinctive phrases: I WALK IN — I SEE YOU — I WATCH YOU — I SCAN YOU — I WAIT FOR YOU — I TEASE YOU — I BREATHE YOU — I SMELL YOU ON MY SKIN. Not only does it attempt to describe the indescribable, it performs the experience of wearing it.

This difference between the surface and what resides just beneath is central to Lang's creative drive. In interview he has

described Vienna as quiet, conservative and mean under a decorative surface. His work can be understood as an attempt to liberate these repressed attributes by embedding them under the supposedly unreadable surface of clothing. Recent advertising campaigns have utilised images from the American photographer Robert Mapplethorpe, whose private portfolio is now as well known as his society portraits and flower studies. Mapplethorpe's depictions of subcultural existence in New York in the 1970s reveal a sparseness of detail and the presence of cloth materials that are very similar to those used by Lang. In using these images for advertising campaigns Lang wishes that the wearing of leather, the baring of skin and the tightness of his clothing be felt through the hard-edged execution of a Mapplethorpe photograph. With 'Man in a Polyester Suit' (see p.44) Lang's suggestion that the surface of clothing is unreadable and commonplace is contradicted by the image itself. The phallic quality of the image reverberates in further Lang campaigns, but it is the tension between the standard exterior and spectacular interior that comes to the fore.

A campaign for Lang's sunglasses range presents the model's face as if photographed for a New York Police Department mugshot, the caption reading 'To promote

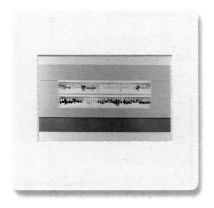

an intellectual and fearless appearance'. In tandem with Mapplethorpe's images we can appreciate how Lang draws from a criminal, medical and individual body of photographic knowledge relating to deviancy to promote the ideal wearer of his clothes. In a sense they are the hardest and most extreme elements of the street, where style is not cultivated but is understood through deviancy as natural, a device curiously oppositional to the artifice of fashion.

As Dutch designers based in Amsterdam, Viktor & Rolf are motivated by their outsider status — outside the stronghold of Parisian couture and the wider fashion system. Their career is symptomatic of the emerging platforms that can support a conceptual approach to fashion: 'Fashion doesn't have to be what people wear. Fashion can be an image.' They are not so interested in the wearing of an image as in how a career in fashion is defined by the status of an image. The couture collections they staged in Paris were produced with the knowledge that they were not only fairly unwearable but also not intended for the women who can afford to buy couture. Instead of residing in salons for sale, these pieces were bought by galleries, museums and fashion institutes and were championed in specialist fashion magazines such as *Visionaire*. The prohibitive expense of *Visionaire* (an issue can cost up to £350)

has ensured that the limited circulation of its images is concurrent with the limited quality of the pieces featured and their archive appeal.

Their Spring/Summer 2001 collection was a review presentation entirely in keeping with the Busby Berkeley production in *Fashions of 1934*, where tap dancers from a Dutch dance academy presented the collection in time to Hollywood musical favourites like 'Singing in the Rain' and 'Forty-second Street'. When the designers took their bow, their appearance centre-stage in white silver-trim blazers, tap shoes and bow-ties not only referenced the tailoring styles on which the womenswear collection was based but also asserted their status, as neither designers nor amateurs but as performers.

In direct contrast the role of Martin Margiela is one played off-stage, made more notorious by his refusal to give interviews. Margiela is best known for his deconstructive clothing, where the marks of his craft — the stitches and seams — are revealed rather than concealed. In being so they display a physical sense of the designer in the construction of the garment and in particular the mark of Margiela's own hand when the garment is presented and animated on the body. The spirit of this approach may be seen in the presentation of the Autumn/Winter

1998–99 collection produced with artist Mark Borthwick and stylist Jane How. How commissioned ten life-size wooden puppets to be dressed in garments from the collection before their animation, by puppeteers, down a staged catwalk. The use of the marionettes in the presentation of the clothes was intimately linked to their construction; the clothes, predominantly T-shirt dresses, had been folded and then heat-bonded to polythene vinyl so that when put on, the neckline and natural fall of the T-shirt material were displaced. Seeing the collection photographically documented in the pages of a catwalk report magazine such as *L'Officiel*, it purposefully jars with the presentation of the human fashion model as the ideal figure striking a pose at the end of the runway.

This idea is taken further in a range of clothes that bear the label Garment Reproduced from a Doll's Wardrobe, where dolls' clothes are scaled to human proportions, creating giant zips and oversize popper fasteners. Margiela points to the slippage between seeing an outfit and wearing it by showing how something is lost and something poetic is found in the translation. His obsession with the animation of objects that pertain to the human form but are not human reveals more than an interest in the artificial and returns to the hand that animates

Helmut Lang
Autumn/Winter 1998–99
'Man in a Polyester Suit 1980'
by Robert Mapplethorpe

The Master of Ceremonies, played
by Anton Walbrook, from Max Ophuls'
La Ronde, 1950

HELMUT LANG

them. In claiming the fashion designer as puppeteer, Margiela suggests a directorial role in shaping the performance that is implicated by the clothes.

The idea of the puppeteer — who gives movement and the appearance of life and was in pagan times an officiating priest — is linked in to the Master of Ceremonies. This is a figure associated with the Expressionist theatre that developed in Germany in the early 1900s, with its concentration on a central figure, an author — hero whose reactions are 'expressed' in the play. For his part the MC manipulates his dummies while indulgently allowing them the illusion of free will. In *La Ronde* (1950, directed by Max Ophuls) the MC is the narrator of a story that concerns a chain of lovers strung together by a series of sexual encounters that are driven by lust across social distinctions. The central motif of the film is a merry-go-round that tunefully turns to a waltz, its sentiment suggesting that all we can do is resign ourselves to continue turning. As a means of presentation for fashion, the merry-go-round is apt: it speaks as much of the process of fashion as it does of the pleasures. (It has also recently been used by Alexander McQueen for his Autumn/Winter 2001–2 collection: see p.98.) Yet perhaps the drive behind this need constantly to turn is powered not by creativity or commerce. In the words of Miuccia Prada: 'Once I asked Louise Bourgeois why people are so much interested in fashion and she said, "It's about seduction." What we might finally ask is not about the source of this desire, its manufacture and motivation, but about the place where we imagine it resides, and the restlessness that makes fashion a constant revolution.

'Style in Revolt'
Hussein Chalayan, Alexander McQueen
& Vivienne Westwood

Valerie Steele

The British have a reputation for being unfashionable, even for hating fashion. It would seem unlikely therefore that much interesting fashion should come out of the United Kingdom. Yet London is regarded as the world's most 'creative' fashion capital. This idea dates from the 1960s, when Swinging London became famous for an emerging youth culture that was characterised by a new style of dress, associated with designers such as Mary Quant, Barbara Hulanicki, and Tuffin & Foale. Yet London had only a moment in the sun, since already by 1964, French designers like André Courrèges and Pierre Cardin were assimilating elements of mod fashion into their work. Although France had no significant youth culture, the metaphor of fashion futurism served in its place. Courrèges even claimed that he, not Mary Quant, had invented the mini-skirt, although Quant more accurately credited the style to the girls in the street.

The next stage of Youthquake fashion emerged from the hippy counterculture. Although London was not central to this social experiment, many young people in the UK were sympathetic to the new style. Indeed, the English had a tradition of bohemian dress going back to the Aesthetic movement of the nineteenth century. By the late 1960s innumerable mods and rockers had transformed into hippies, at least as far as their appearance was concerned. Hippy anti-fashion was perceived as even more radical than the previous youth styles, because it signalled allegiance to a new set of values, which ranged from the hedonistic (sex, drugs and rock'n'roll) to the more overtly political. Notwithstanding the anti-capitalist rhetoric of the hippies, the new style of clothing inevitably became a commodity. Initially created by trendsetting designers such as Ossie Clark, the style was assimilated into the fashion system at all levels. French designers such as Yves Saint Laurent brought hippy-inspired fashion to the haute couture, while American manufacturers churned it out for the masses. By the 1970s, London's fashion leadership had become a thing of the past. Not only had Paris largely regained its reputation for high fashion but Milan was emerging as the next fashion capital on the basis of its luxurious modern sportswear.

The punk subculture of the late 1970s and 1980s put London back on the map. The designer most closely associated with punk was Vivienne Westwood, who became notorious for her pornographic T-shirts and bondage trousers. As cultural critic Dick Hebdige famously observed in *Subculture: The Meaning of Style*, the punk 'style in revolt' was a deliberately 'revolting style' — although this did not keep it from becoming a major influence on fashion, both at the time and repeatedly since then. Westwood's 'confrontation dressing' captured the essence of the punk look, with its mix of sex and aggression. But as punk began to mutate into other subcultures, such as new romanticism, Westwood's work continued to evolve. Her famous Pirates collection of 1981, for example, epitomised her belief in looking to the history of the world for powerful design ideas. By the mid-80s she had revived the corset, introduced underwear-as-outerwear and invented the mini-crini. Westwood increasingly referenced history and high culture rather than street style. Yet despite her enthusiasm for traditional sartorial status symbols (Harris tweed jackets, tartan, twinsets), her designs remained deeply eccentric and implicitly subversive. Westwood's influence on other designers was considerable. Not only did she inspire Zandra Rhodes' famous Conceptual Chic collection, but European designers as different as Jean Paul Gaultier and Christian Lacroix owed much to her. For younger British designers, in particular, she was an iconic figure. Nevertheless, for many years Westwood struggled to

Vivienne Westwood,
Portrait Collection, Autumn/Winter 1990
(photo: Niall McInerney)

keep her business going, even as other designers capitalised on her design innovations. Nor was this difficulty unique to Westwood. Many observers believe that one of the most serious problems facing British fashion is the lack of a strong infrastructure comparable to those in place in France and Italy. For although the system of design education in Great Britain is admired throughout the world, many fashion students have only been able to find good jobs abroad. The most famous example of this is John Galliano, who first exploded on to the scene with his 1984 degree collection from Central St Martin's. This collection, Les Incroyables, inspired by the French Revolution, was immediately purchased and displayed in the influential London boutique Browns. Galliano rapidly gained a cult following, but financial backers came and went, and eventually he decamped to Paris. As late as 1994, it was unclear whether Galliano would be able to succeed, but with the help of Anna Wintour, the British-born editor-in-chief of American *Vogue*, he found enough money to produce a small collection, which was presented in the Parisian townhouse of socialite Sao Schlumberger.

Galliano's collection was well received by both press and buyers, which led to his appointment in 1995 as head designer of Givenchy. Two years on he moved to the even more prestigious house of Christian Dior. With financial backing from luxury conglomorate LVMH, he was also able to continue his own fashion company. Like Westwood, Galliano is obsessed with fashion history, creating designs that Richard Martin, one-time curator of the Costume Institute at the Metropolitan Museum of Art, once described as a 'fantastic pastiche'. A romantic fantasist, Galliano has drawn on fashions as disparate as those of eighteenth-century France and Shanghai in the 1930s. Aesthetic influences from East Africa and Burma are applied to a sartorial skeleton deriving from Belle Epoque Paris. In another collection, Galliano's vision of Native American culture seems to have arrived by way of the Indians in Peter Pan.

The theatrical element in Galliano's vision is central, although it frequently causes controversy. A collection inspired by the homeless aroused great anger in Paris, while a fetish collection shocked Americans. The Spring/Summer 2001 show for Dior, dubbed 'Anarchic Chic' by the press, opened with a sound track repeating an obscene word for the female genitals. Fashion journalists were more annoyed, however, when Galliano's own collection proved to be essentially a repeat performance of the Dior show. Andrew Tucker's book on London fashion suggests that, despite the fact that Galliano is based in Paris, there is something peculiarly British about the way he absorbs 'wildly diverging historical and cultural elements to invent new hybridisations of the contemporary'. Galliano himself insists that 'Creativity has no nationality' (Tucker, 1998). Yet it does seem, at the very least, that Westwood's version of British fashion has exerted a powerful influence on Galliano.

No sooner had Galliano achieved fame and fortune than a new contender to the throne of British fashion appeared in Alexander McQueen. Born in East London, the son of a taxi driver, McQueen left school at sixteen. Although he had always been obsessed with drawing clothes, it was only when his mother saw a programme on television about how tailors on Savile Row needed apprentices that he began to learn about construction. After working at bespoke tailors Anderson & Sheppard for two years, he moved on to Gieves & Hawkes. To this day, McQueen is known for his exceptional tailoring skills. Next he worked for the theatrical costumiers Berman & Nathan, followed by a brief period with Koji Tatsuno, a designer who combined traditional British tailoring with avant-garde design. After Koji Tatsuno went bankrupt, the 20-year-old McQueen bought a one-way ticket to Milan and presented himself at the atelier of Romeo Gigli, where he worked for almost a year. Coming back to London, he applied for a position teaching pattern-cutting at

Central St Martin's. Impressed by his drive and talent, the college offered him the opportunity to study in its prestigious postgraduate fashion-design programme. His degree collection was bought by Isabella Blow, then fashion editor at British *Vogue*, who began to promote McQueen. From his first show, Highland Rape, McQueen has been at the centre of controversy. The tabloid press characterised him as a working-class lout, a 'yob among snobs', an impression fed by McQueen's often provocative remarks.

Yet McQueen was always more complex than he seemed. Despite the impression created by models staggering on stage in ripped tartan garments, his 1995 Highland Rape collection was inspired by the 'rape' of Scotland by the British. As he said in an interview with Susannah Frankel in *The Independent Magazine* ('The Real McQueen', 8 Sept 1999), 'The reason I'm patriotic about Scotland is because I think it's been dealt a really hard hand ... There's nothing romantic about its history. What the British did there was nothing short of genocide.' Later collections also focused on the place where sex and violence meet. But commentators who accuse McQueen of misogyny are mistaken, he argues. As an eight year old, he saw his sister's husband brutally attacking her, and ever since he has been aware of the way women are treated. 'Everything I've done was for the purpose of making women look stronger.'

First dubbed the 'bad boy of British fashion', he was later touted as a 'genius', two clichés that avoid addressing his contributions to fashion, which are considerable. The first thing people notice are his shows, widely acknowledged to be the world's most exciting. The Hunger (Spring/Summer 1996) featured clothing and jewellery that evoked themes of bondage and decay. Dante (Autumn/Winter 1996) alluded to sexual perversion and fetish worship, as models appeared masked, wearing corsets, and adorned with animal parts and crucifixes. The very beautiful clothes in Bellmer's La Poupée (Spring/Summer 1997) were worn by models who walked through water, often in manacles; one model restricted by a metal harness that forced her body into a crab-like position. A model for Untitled (Spring/Summer 1998) had what looked like a bit between her teeth. One of McQueen's most spectacular shows was Joan (Autumn/ Winter 1998), which took as its inspiration the story of Joan of Arc. Beginning with a model wearing a short silver dress, like chain-mail armour for a woman warrior, the show moved inexorably toward a fiery end. An impeccably tailored red jacket flared open over the model's bosom. A long black jacket lined with red was shown on a model wearing red contact lenses. A reddish-black pantsuit with a long jacket gave way to sparkling red trousers and a black corset worn over a sheer blouse. A long black coat was buttoned tightly over a red dress, alluding both to saintly asceticism and hell fire. A red lace dress was rendered mysterious with red lace-work over the head and face. A man in red and black resembled a nightmare vision of the executioner. The show concluded with a girl in a red fringed dress being enveloped in flames.

The drama of the presentation is in no way extraneous to the clothes. All of McQueen's strengths as a designer are on display, especially his surgical tailoring, which both sexualises the body and clothes the wearer in power. The same tension between sexuality and violence came to the fore when McQueen art-directed an issue of *Dazed & Confused* about models with severe physical disabilities. Although McQueen was accused of sensationalism and exploitation, the result was far from being a freak show. One of the models, Aimee Mullens, whose legs had been amputated from the knees down, appeared on his catwalk wearing hand-carved legs, an event that came across as inclusive and empowering. At the age of 27, after having presented only eight collections of his own, McQueen was chosen to replace

John Galliano at Givenchy. (Galliano then moved to Christian Dior.) Greeted with trepidation, McQueen truculently told the press: 'I don't give a shit what other French designers think of me, I'll bring French chic to Paris.' Over the next few years his employers at Givenchy often seemed unsure about him, and there were rumours that he would be fired. Certainly, his hard-edged chic was at odds with the restrained French elegance that had characterised the house under its founder, Hubert de Givenchy. Although many of his collections for Givenchy were outstanding, McQueen's own label remained as dangerously under funded as it was cutting edge. Recently, though, Gucci has placed its financial clout behind McQueen's eponymous collection.

McQueen is today widely regarded as the king of British fashion. Who could forget the sight of robotic arms borrowed from Fiat spraying paint on Shalom Harlow (see p.101)? Yet he has moved beyond the stereotype of British fashion as fantastic 'dress up'. Unlike Westwood and Galliano, there are few obvious his-toricising elements in his work. Nor is it particularly inspired by the London club scene, although, like street style, his design embraces sexual fetishism and body modification. It is, of course, theatrical and transgressive in ways that are regarded as typically British, much like the new Brit-pack art. McQueen is

a provocateur. But his work also draws on the best traditions of Savile Row.

Hussein Chalayan is a very different type of designer, cerebral where McQueen is theatrical, austere and architectural where McQueen is wild and sexy. Chalayan has been stereotyped as a 'difficult', 'intellectual' designer. It is true that the concept is as important to him as the clothes. He reads philosophy and history, and creates collections inspired by religion, isolation and oppression. If his work is radical, this is precisely because it draws on the same sources as avant-garde art. The only child of Turkish Cypriot parents, Chalayan was born in Nicosia in 1970. Although his childhood was in many ways idyllic, he was aware that Cyprus was a divided society, with Christian Greeks pitted against Muslim Turks and, in a sense, men against women. 'I love women,' says Chalayan in interview with Susannah Frankel ('A Prize Fighter', *Independent Magazine*, Spring/Summer 2000). 'I was brought up by women. In a way, it's the fact that my mother, growing up where she did, had so few opportunities, that has made me ambi-tious. I wanted to make the best out of any talent or any passion I might have.' His parents separated when he was twelve years old, and he left behind 'the sweetest of mothers' to go to England with his father. He considered studying architecture

but changed to fashion design because he was interested in creating objects intimately associated with the body. At Central St Martin's, he was different from the other fashion students, seldom looking at fashion magazines, and more interested in ideas than in clothes per se. One tutor supposedly told him to 'bugger off and study sculpture'. Nevertheless, he pursued his unorthodox vision. For his 1993 degree collection he buried the clothing in a friend's backyard and sprinkled iron filings on it to see how it rusted and decomposed. The collection was shown in the windows of Browns, just as Galliano's Incroyables had been almost a decade earlier.

Chalayan's fashion shows resemble performance art or installations more than the conventional catwalk. 'The way he presents his work is ground-breaking,' says Lucille Lewin (Mark Holgate, 'Outsider Edge', British *Vogue*, November 1998). Lewin has bought all of his collections for Whistles. 'It's never just a designer showing clothes on the catwalk, or even an indulgent designer showing "art". During Panoramic, I sat there thinking, Is this the kind of thrill I would have got watching one of Diaghilev's productions earlier this century?' Between (Spring/Summer 1998) famously portrayed women in Muslim body coverings that revealed progressively more of their naked bodies, until only the face was veiled. Shock value

Alexander McQueen
Silver Coin Dress and Embroidered
Head Piece, Spring/Summer 2000
(photo: Chris Moore)

was not the point. Although not personally religious, he is interested in religion, especially its impact on people's lives. By staging an event like this show, he forced people to think about religion, the body and women's position in society.

For Chalayan the body has cultural connotations. Yet his clothes are not sexy, nor does he want them to be. 'Sex has always sold fashion, and I'm just tired of it ... Sexiness doesn't come from what you wear... it's all to do with feeling good about yourself' (as he continues in 'Outsider Edge'). Often his clothes are thought provoking. For example, whereas many other designers create sexy corsets that evoke an idealised shape, Chalayan made a surgical corset that alludes to the idea of a body that is wounded and vulnerable. Another of his corsets was made of polished wood that bolted closed. Space is also central to his vision: clothing is an intimate zone around the body, architecture is a larger one. It also exists as territory, from which refugees can be expelled, taking with them only a few possessions. After Words (Autumn/Winter 2000) opened on a set arranged to look like a living room, but the furniture covers became dresses, and the table was transformed into a skirt. Space also interacts with time, while culture and technology act on nature. A fibreglass dress opens electronically. Fascinated by flight, Chalayan's

Temporary Interference (Summer 1995) included prints based on the images on an air-traffic controller's screen. Scenes of Tempest (Winter 1997) used patterning based on meteorological charts, reflecting Chalayan's vision of weather as a god or natural force. His collection Airmail Clothing (1999) was made from non-rip paper that could be folded into envelopes and sent through the mail.

Chalayan likes to call himself an ideas, not a fashion, person. Whether or not people understand Chalayan's ideas is immaterial; he believes they are vital to the creative process. As for the clothes: 'The final result is minimal,' he says, but not, 'in terms of the research and thought that has gone into it.' He is understandably dismayed when people assume that his clothes are difficult. In fact, they are deceptively simple and gentle, with well-articulated but minimal silhouettes. The purity and serenity of the designs is striking. 'Do you consider yourself to be an English designer?' reporters ask ('Architecte du corps', *Beaux-Arts*, March 1999). 'No,' Chalayan replies flatly (in an echo of what Constance White reports him as saying in 'Hussein Chalayan's High-wire Act', *New York Times*, 21 April 1998). 'I'm Turkish-Cypriot ... not British. The only thing that makes a certain thing British is the different influences, being provocative, doing youthful looks. I don't belong to any of those really.'

Within the world of fashion certain characteristics are popularly associated with various 'national' styles. Thus British fashion is perceived as 'eccentric' and/or closely related to subcultural or street styles. As Chalayan suggests, British designers are known for their youthful, provocative creativity, much as British artists tend to be stereotyped as sensational and young. However, this is an oversimplification. Within both fields the very idea of national character has been largely discredited. Certainly, a designer like Alexander McQueen has more in common with, say, Jean Paul Gaultier than with Hussein Chalayan, while Chalayan has more in common with Rei Kawakubo than with anyone working in London. Radical fashion is valuable precisely because it raises questions about concepts too often taken for granted. As we travel from New York to London, Paris and Milan, or when we look at Belgian or Japanese fashion, we need to remind ourselves that national labels are useful only to a degree. They can also blind us to the particularities of certain designers' work or their connections across cultures. Similarly, we may not know exactly what we mean by 'radical fashion', but we still need to explore why certain fashions go beyond conventional commercial design, moving toward an unknown future.

The Designers

Azzedine Alaïa

*'When I see beautiful clothes, I want to keep them, preserve them…
clothes, like architecture and art, reflect an era.'*

Azzedine Alaïa
Jacket with Broderie Anglaise | Spring/Summer 1992
Photo: Hamid Bechiri

Azzedine Alaïa

Bandage Dress series: the violet dress was made for Grace Jones for the Fashion Oscars 1985 | Spring/Summer 1985 — Spring/Summer 1990

Photo: Hamid Bechiri

Azzedine Alaïa
Shirt with Broderie Anglaise and Openwork Leather Corset Belt | Spring/Summer 1992
Photo: Hamid Bechiri

Azzedine Alaïa
Evening Dress in Black Silk Faille | Autumn/Winter 2000–01
Photo: Hamid Bechiri

Azzedine Alaïa
Pleated Jersey Dress with Black Leather Skirt and Straps | Autumn/Winter 1979
Photo: Hamid Bechiri

Azzedine Alaïa
White Cotton Dress in Broderie Anglaise | Spring/Summer 1992
Photo: Hamid Bechiri

Azzedine Alaïa
Black Silk Chiffon Dress Embroidered with Gold Pearls, made for Tina Turner | Spring/Summer 1989
Photo: Hamid Bechiri

63

Hussein Chalayan

'I really do think I'm an ideas person. People often don't realise that whatever an idea is, ideas are always valuable. There's something to be respected in every given idea, no matter where it comes from.'

Hussein Chalayan
Memory Denim, Echoform | Autumn/Winter 1999
Photo: Marcus Tomlinson

Hussein Chalayan
Wooden Conehead, Between | Spring/Summer 1998
Art Direction: Matthias Vriens | Photo: Pierre Paradis

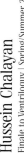

Hussein Chalayan
Tulle Dress, Before Minus Now | Spring/Summer 2000
Photo: Chris Moore

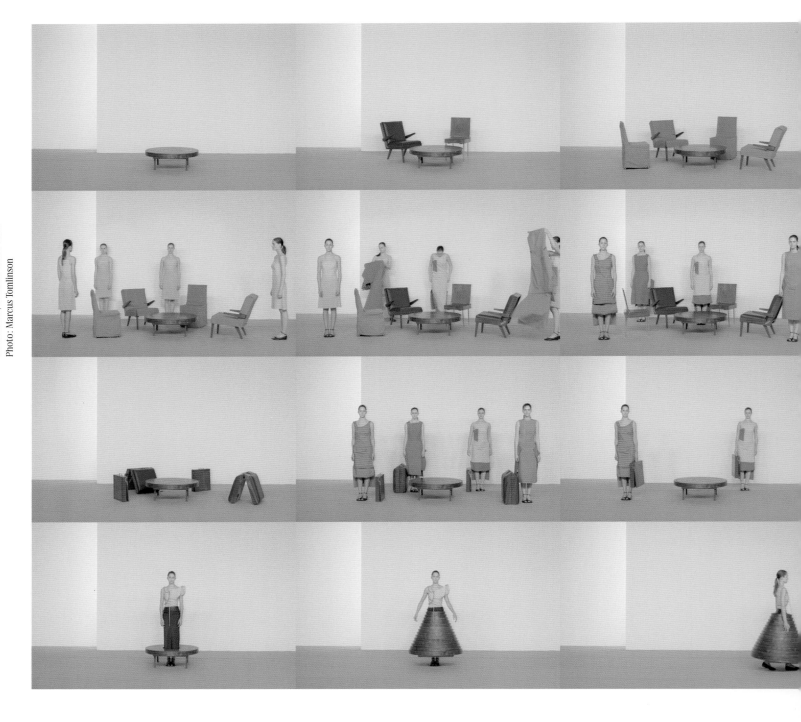

Hussein Chalayan
Poppy Dress, Ventriloquy | Spring/Summer 2001
Photo: Chris Moore

Comme des Garçons

'I try to make clothes that are new, that didn't exist before, and hope that people get energy and feel positive when they wear them. I believe that creativity is an essential part of life.'

Rei Kawakubo

Jean Paul Gaultier

'I like my clothes to take a lot of different influences and to show them together.
So there is not one kind of beauty but many kinds of beauty.'

Jean Paul Gaultier
Durbar: Camouflage Dress in Silk Tulle | Haute Couture Spring/Summer 2000
Model: Natalia Z | Photo: Patrice Stable

Jean Paul Gaultier

Café de Paris: Pleated Bronze Jersey Sweater, Mink Bolero, Brown Leather Trousers | Haute Couture Autumn/Winter 2000–01

Photo: Patrice Stable

Jean Paul Gaultier
Paris sous la Pluie: Off-white Kilt Trench in Wool, Brown Leather Dress and Umbrella Bag | Haute Couture Autumn/Winter 2000–01
Model: Erin Wasson | Photo: Patrice Stable

Jean Paul Gaultier
Srinagar: Sweater Dress in Pleated Black Silk Tulle and Long Skirt in Black Silk Jersey | Haute Couture Spring/Summer 2000
Model: Julia | Photo: Patrice Stable

Jean Paul Gaultier

Himalaya: White Silk Tulle Coat with Pale Green Jersey Dress | Haute Couture Spring/Summer 2000
Model: Chrystelle Saint Louis | Photo: Patrice Stable

Jean Paul Gaultier

Feux de Bengale: Organdie Sheath Dress | Haute Couture Spring/Summer 2001
Model: Chrystelle Saint Louis | Photo: Patrice Stable

Jean Paul Gaultier

Paris dans Chaque Faubourg: Black Wool Jacket, Trousers and Tie, Brown Veil | Haute Couture Autumn/Winter 2000–01
Model: Alek Wek | Photo: Patrice Stable

Helmut Lang

'It's about the known unknown and the unknown known.'

HELMUT LANG

est. 1986

FINEST CLOTHING AND LUXURY GOODS FOR MEN AND WOMEN
AVAILABLE WORLDWIDE **WWW.HELMUTLANG.COM** NEW YORK N.Y. - S/S 01
NEW YORK PARIS VIENNA MUNICH MILAN TOKYO KOBE HONG KONG SINGAPORE LONDON LOS ANGELES SAN FRANCISCO

Helmut Lang
Menswear advertisement, When Love Comes to Town | Spring/Summer 2001
Photo: Inez van Lamsweerde & Vinoodh Matadin

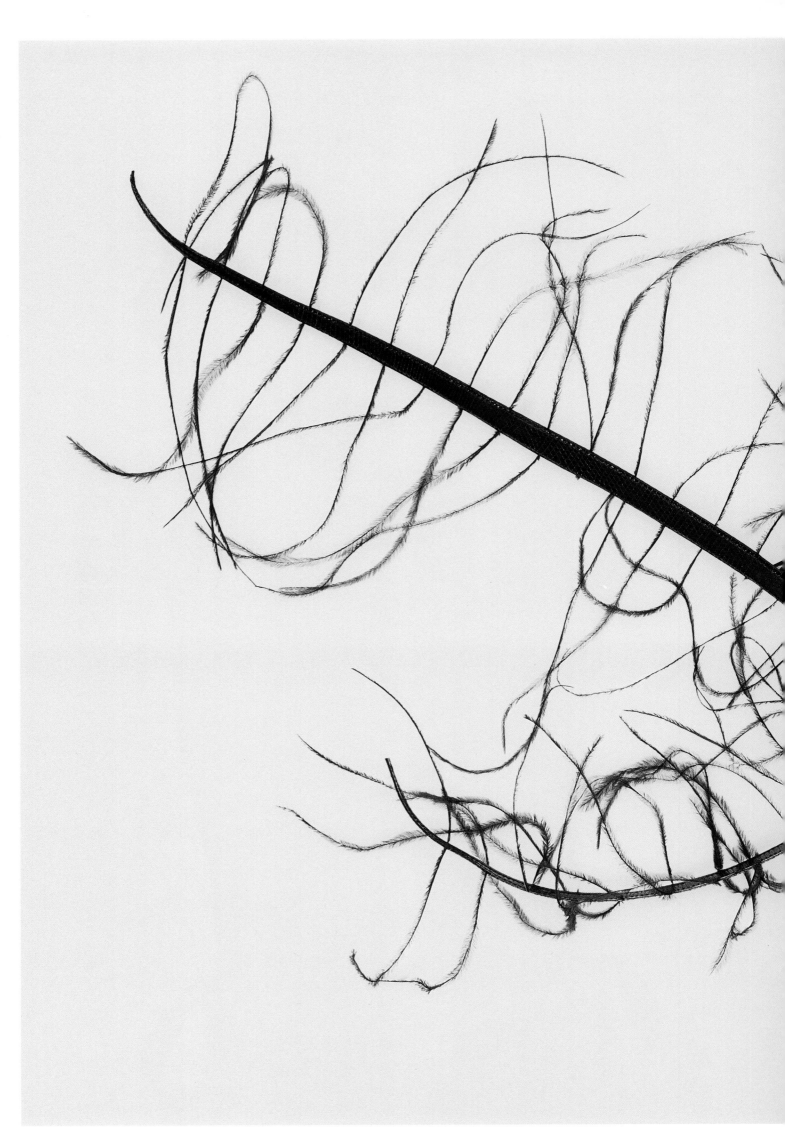

Helmut Lang
Womenswear advertisement, Black Lizard and Feather Boa, When Love Comes to Town | Spring/Summer 2001
Photo: Anthony Ward

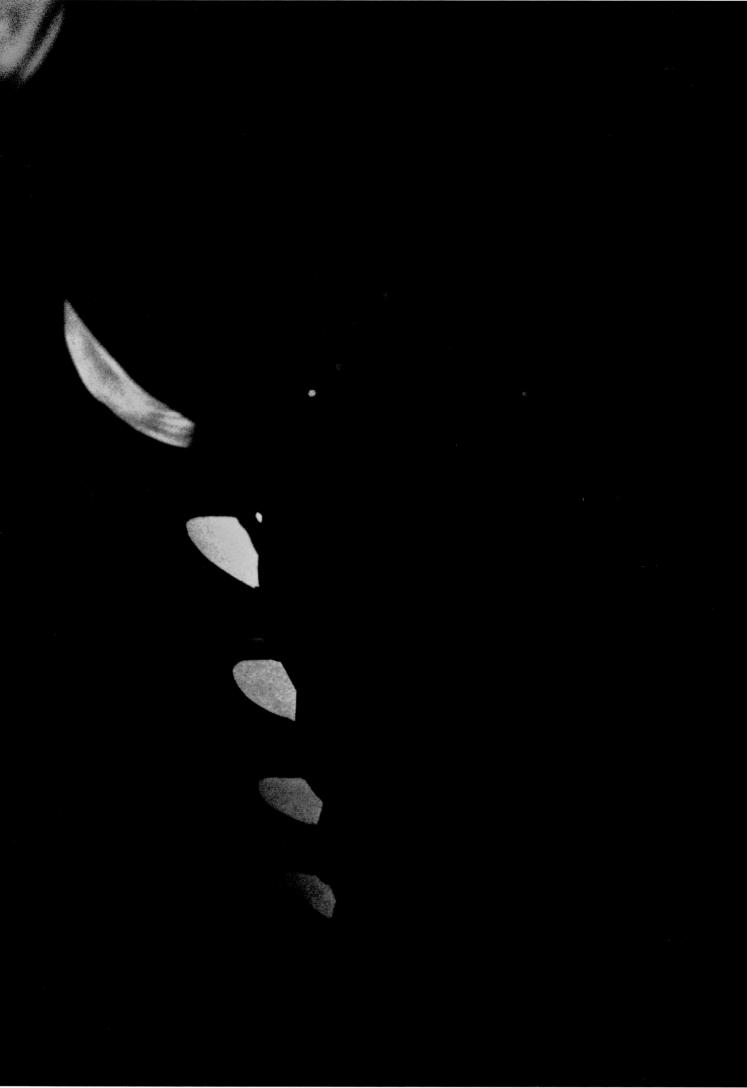

Helmut Lang
Holes, When Love Comes to Town | Spring/Summer 2001
Photo: Elfie Semotan

Helmut Lang
Watercolour on paper, Kurt Kocherscheidt, 1992

Helmut Lang
Torso, When Love Comes to Town | Spring/Summer 2001
Photo: Inez van Lamsweerde & Vinoodh Matadin

Helmut Lang
Watercolour on paper, Kurt Kocherscheidt, 1992

Alexander McQueen

'There's beauty in anger, and anger for me is a passion.'

Alexander McQueen

Wooden Fan Jacket by Givenchy Haute Couture, S/S 1998, Suede T-shirt by Alexander McQueen; crinoline frame from Angels & Bermans
Model: Aimee Mullens | Art Direction: Alexander McQueen for *Dazed & Confused*, Sept. 1998 | Photo: Nick Knight

Alexander McQueen

Green Lace Embroidered Dress, Green-grey Sash and Rosette, What a Merry-Go-Round | Autumn/Winter 2001

Model: Miki Olin | Photo: Chris Moore

Alexander McQueen
Razor-shell Dress, Voss 2001 | Spring/Summer 2001
Model: Erin O'Connor | Photo: Chris Moore

Alexander McQueen
Backstage shot of Red-glass Slide and Ostrich Feather Dress, Voss 2001 | Spring/Summer 2001
Model: Erin O'Connor | Photo: Anne Deniau

Alexander McQueen
White Sprayed Dress with Tan Leather Belt, # 13 | Spring/Summer 1999
Model: Shalom Harlow | Photo: Anne Deniau

Alexander McQueen
Swarovski Black Mesh and Crystal Dress with Cube Hat by Philip Treacy for Alexander McQueen, # 13 | Spring/Summer 1999
Model: Esther Cañadas | Photo: Anne Deniau

Alexander McQueen
Metal Skirt and Leather Top, The Overlook | Autumn/Winter 1999
Model: Diana Gartner | Photo: Chris Moore

Maison Martin Margiela

*'Fashion is an inspiration, a craft, a technical know-how and not,
in our opinion, an art form.'*

Maison Martin Margiela

Heavy Grey Wool Pea Coat, Italian size 42 enlarged 150 per cent, Sernam | Autumn/Winter 2000–01
Art Direction: Maison Martin Margiela | Photo: Marina Faust | First published in *The Fashion*

150%

Maison Martin Margiela
Hand-painted Black Frame Sunglasses, 148 per cent of original size | Spring/Summer 2000
Art Direction: Maison Martin Margiela | Photo: Marina Faust | First published in *The Fashion*

148%

100% 200%

Maison Martin Margiela

1960s Cocktail Dress, cut and enlarged by 200 per cent | Spring/Summer 2000
Art Direction: Maison Martin Margiela | Photo: Marina Faust | First published in *The Fashion*

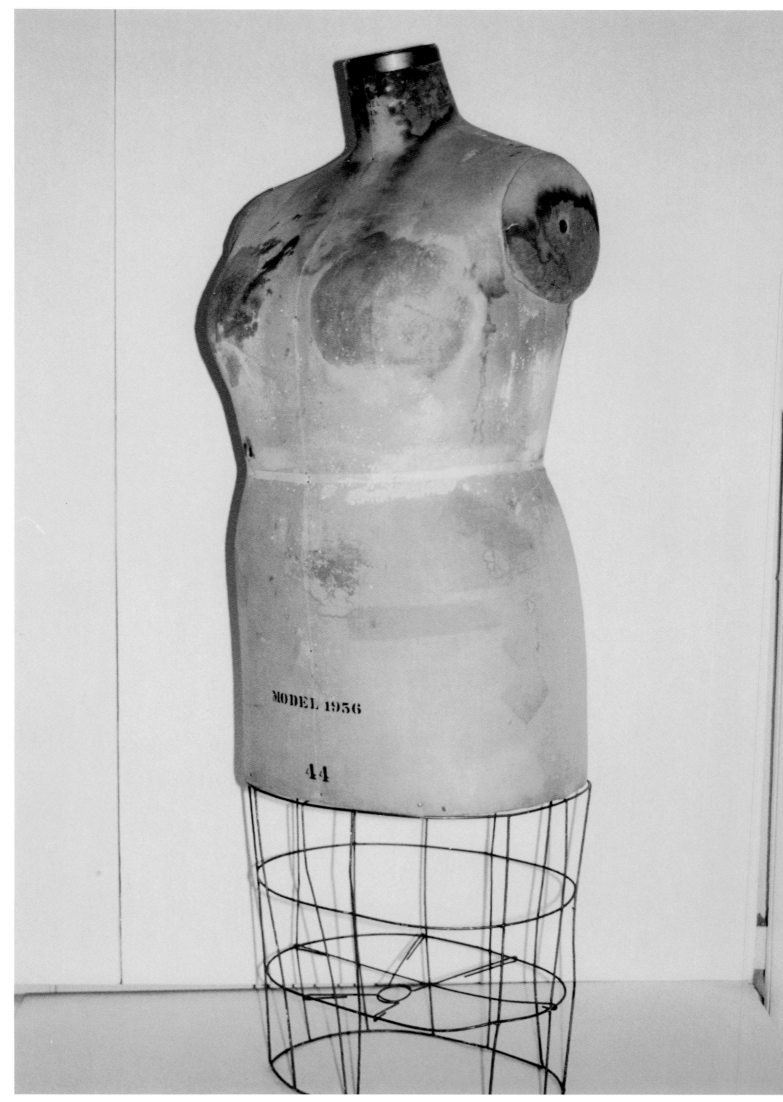

MODEL 1956

44

Maison Martin Margiela

Sleeveless Jacket of a Two-piece Suit, enlarged 148 per cent, March 2000 with protective white-silk paper | Autumn/Winter 2000–01
Art Direction: Maison Martin Margiela | Photo: Marina Faust | First published in *The Fashion*

148%

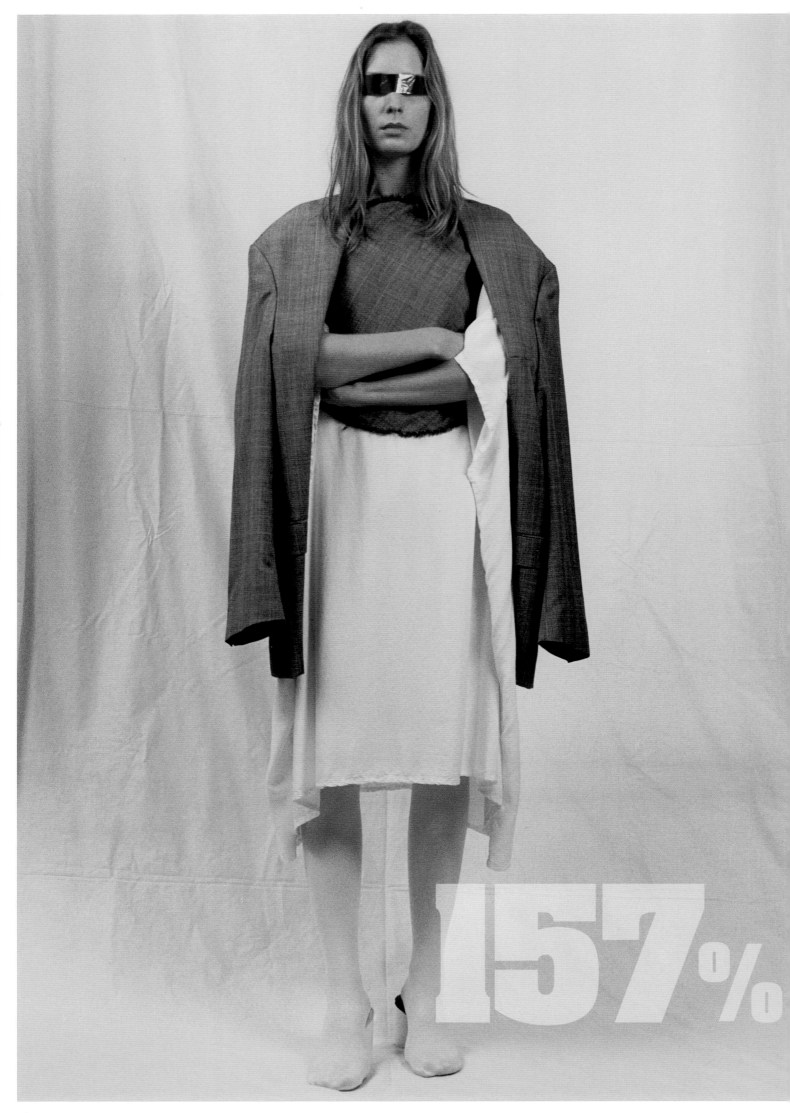

Maison Martin Margiela
Prince of Wales Check Jacket, enlarged 157 per cent, White Rectangular 'Tent' Dress with Appliquéd Suiting Fabric | Spring/Summer 2001
Art Direction: Maison Martin Margiela | Photo: Marina Faust | First published in *The Fashion*

Maison Martin Margiela

Destroyed Jeans, Italian size 42, enlarged 200 per cent | Autumn/Winter 2000–01
Art Direction: Maison Martin Margiela | Photo: Marina Faust | First published in *The Fashion*

Issey Miyake

*'Sometimes my clothes are radical, probably sometimes challenging,
but I try not to fear radical things.'*

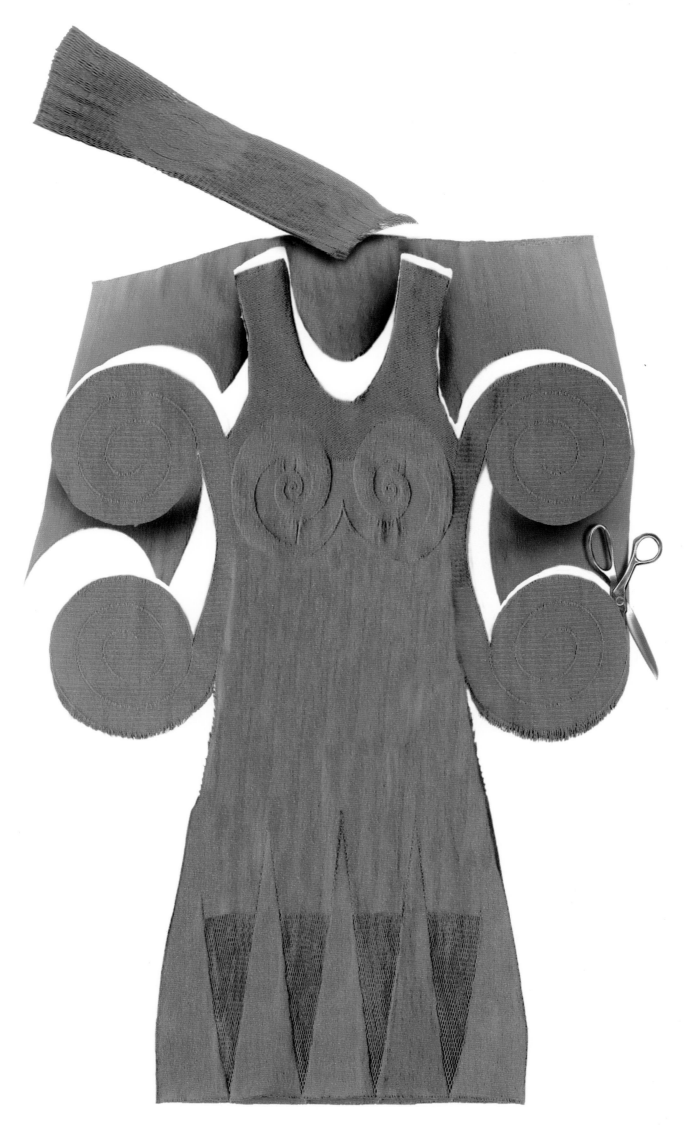

Issey Miyake
One Piece, A-POC | 2001
Brochure: Pascal Goulin

Issey Miyake
A-POC | 1999 (from Issey Miyake Making Things, ACE Gallery, New York, November 1999)
Photo: Yasuaki Yoshinaga

Issey Miyake
Just Before and A-POC | 2000 (from Issey Miyake Making Things, Museum of Contemporary Art, Tokyo, April 2000)
Photo: S.Anzaï

115

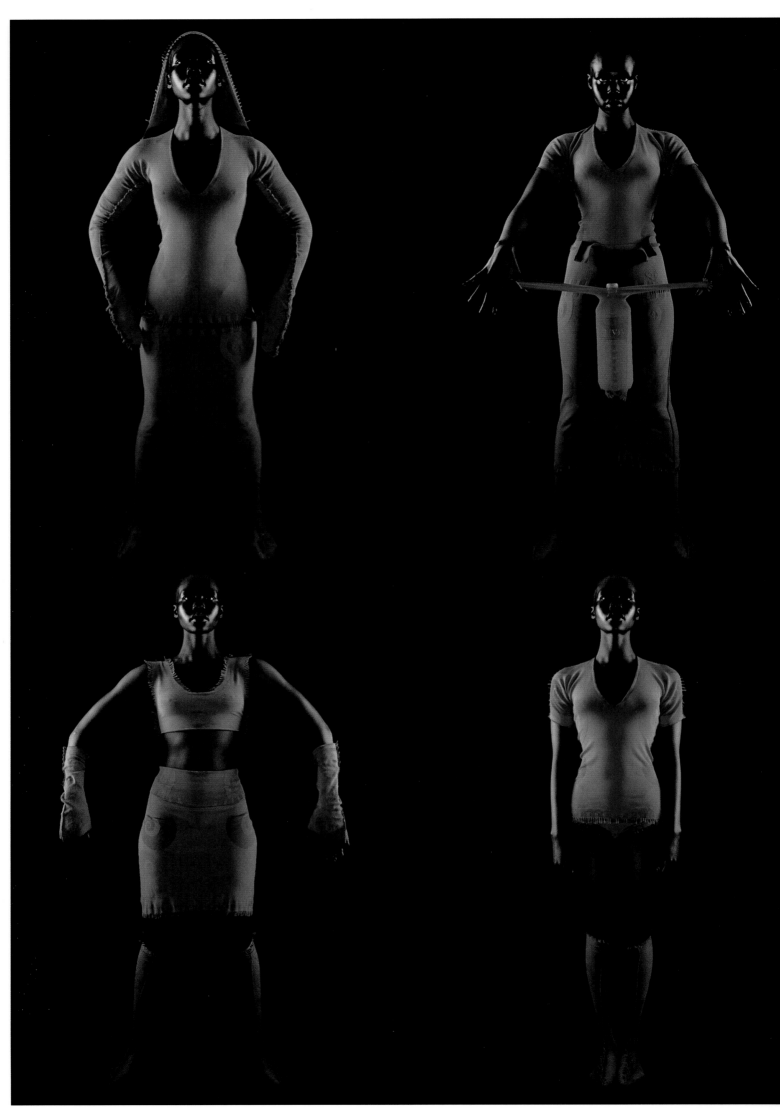

Issey Miyake
Green Queen, A-POC | 1999
Photo: Sandro Sodano

117

Issey Miyake
A-POC Knit, A-POC | 2000
Photo: Friedemann Hauss

Issey Miyake
Jeux de Tissu performance by Yayoi kusuma on A-POC King and Queen | 2000
Photo: Friedemann Hauss

Junya Watanabe Comme des Garçons

'We move on by believing in our ideas.'

Junya Watanabe

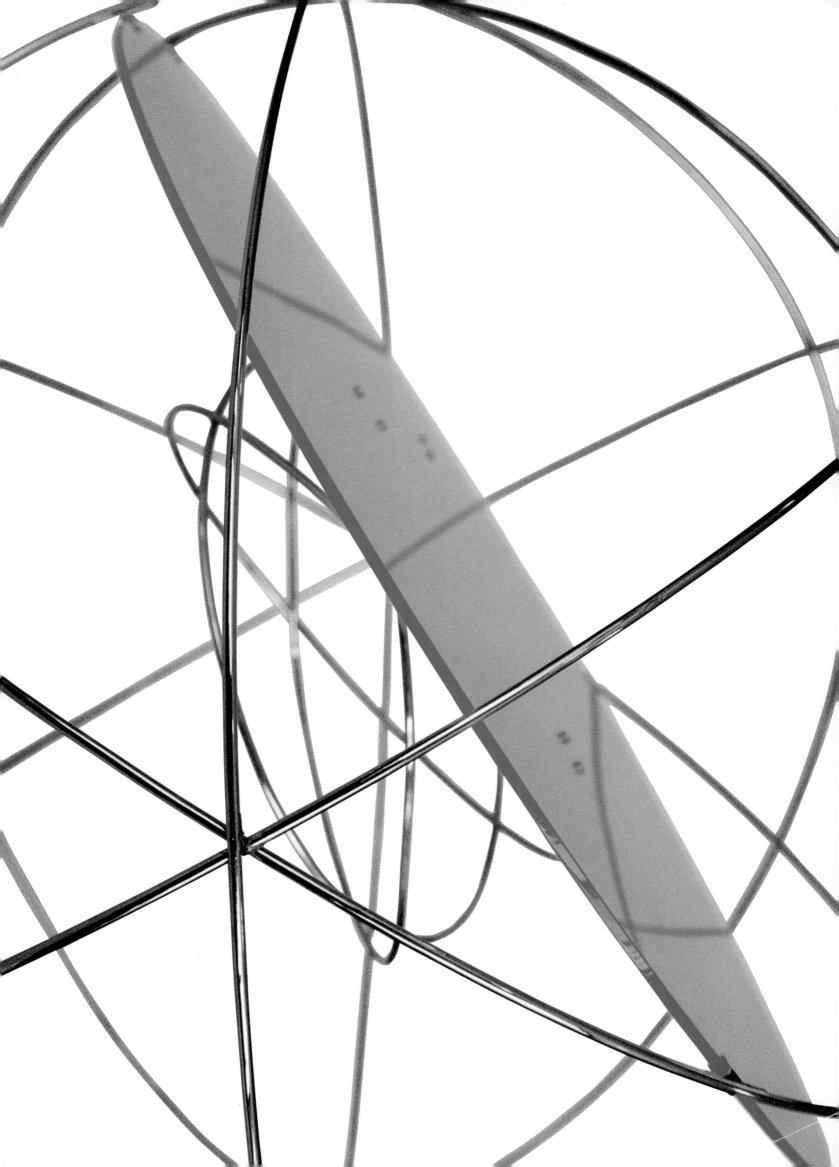

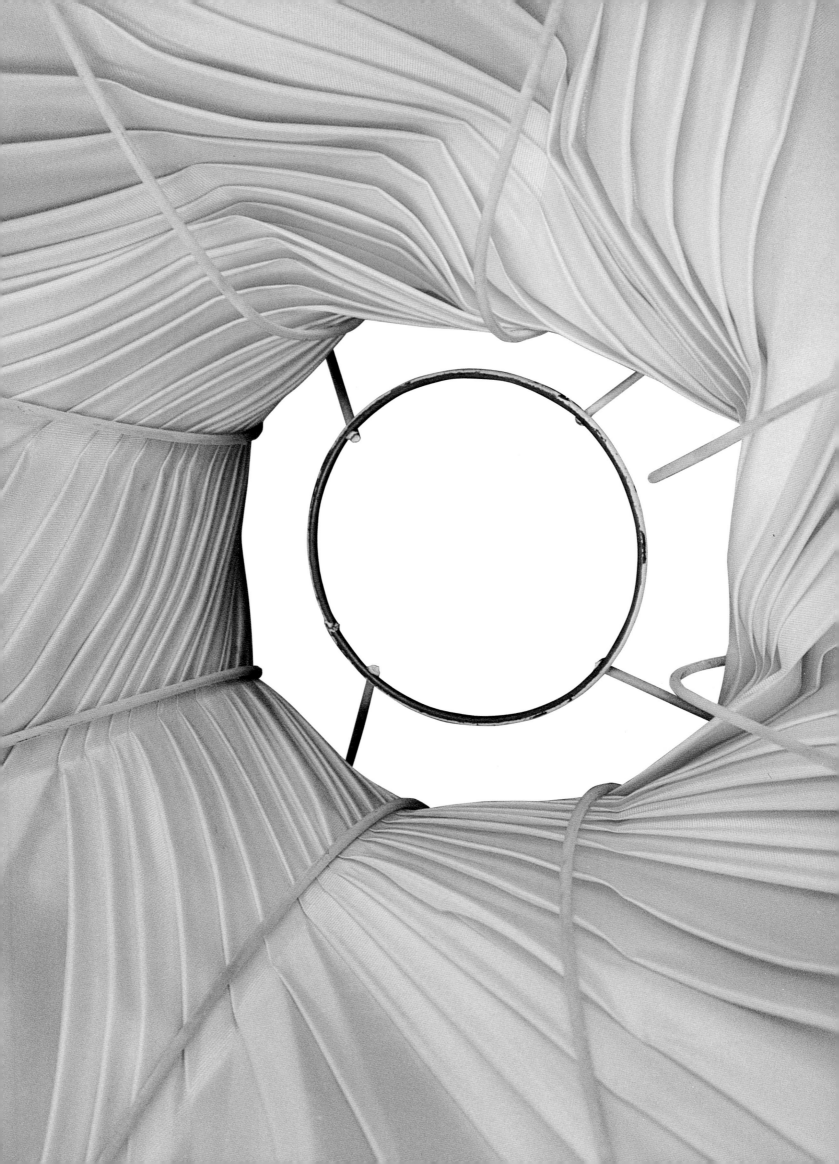

Vivienne Westwood

'As soon as you begin to use a word like "radical" to describe fashion you are faced with a paradox: in order to do anything original you have to build it on tradition.'

Vivienne Westwood
Vivienne Red 'Portrait' Jacket and Slashed Leather Statue of Liberty Corset, Dressing Up | Autumn/Winter 1991
Photo: Chris Moore

Vivienne Westwood

Silk Flower Print Strapless Statue of Liberty Dress and Matching Sleeves worn with 'Animal' Trousers, Exploration | Spring/Summer 2001

Photo: Ugo Camera

Vivienne Westwood

Cotton Stripe 'Saville' Jacket and Shorts over Sun Print T-shirt, Exploration | Spring/Summer 2001
Photo: Ugo Camera

Vivienne Westwood
Distressed Denim Overall, Man | Autumn/Winter 2001–02
Photo: Ugo Camera

Vivienne Westwood
Beaded Cricket Vest and Flannel Pants, Man | Autumn/Winter 2001–02
Photo: Ugo Camera

Vivienne Westwood
Grey Wool 'Metropolitan' Suit, Vive La Cocotte | Autumn/Winter 1995
Model: Naomi Campbell | Photo: Chris Moore

Yohji Yamamoto

'I'm not a couturier, I'm a cutter.'

Yohji Yamamoto
Red and Black Hat, Black Frockcoat and Trousers | Autumn/Winter 1985–86
Model: Sasha Robertson | Art Direction: Marc Ascoli | Photo: Paolo Roversi

Yohji Yamamoto
Wool Frockcoats with Bustlebacks | Autumn/Winter 1986–87
Art Direction: Marc Ascoli | Graphics: Peter Saville | Photo: Nick Knight

Yohji Yamamoto
Red Worsted Wool Coat Layered with Fine Net | Autumn/Winter 1995–96
Model: Stella Tennant | Art Direction: Marc Ascoli | Design: M/M | Photo: David Sims

Yohji Yamamoto
White Cotton Shirt, Summer Wool Jacket | Spring/Summer 1997
Model: Guinevere van Seenus | Art Direction & Design: M/M | Photo: Paolo Roversi

Yohji Yamamoto
'Cloud' Hat, Black Rayon Dress with Twisted Detail | Spring/Summer 1998
Model: Maggie Rizzer | Art Direction & Design: M/M | Photo: Inez van Lamsweerde & Vinoodh Matadin

Yohji Yamamoto
Reversible Fitted Coat with Net Yokes | Autumn/Winter 1995–96
Model: Stella Tennant | Art Direction: Marc Ascoli | Design: M/M | Photography: David Sims

Yohji Yamamoto
Black Cotton Jersey Bustier Dress with Inflatable Skirt under Jersey Wrap Skirt, Black Velvet Hat, Mariage | Spring/Summer 1999
Model: Hannelore | Art Direction & Design: M/M | Photo: Inez van Lamsweerde & Vinoodh Matadin

Bibliography

Barthes, Roland, *The Fashion System* (trans. M. Ward & R. Howard; U. of California Press, Berkeley, 1990)

Baudot, Francois, *Yohji Yamamoto* (Thames & Hudson, London, 1997)

Benstock, Shari, & Ferriss, Suzanne (eds), *On Fashion* (Rutgers U. Press, New Jersey, 1994)

Bolton, Andrew, *The Supermodern Wardrobe* (V&A, London, forthcoming)

Braddock, Sarah, E., & O'Mahoney, Marie, *Techno Textiles: Revolutionary Fabrics for Fashion and Design* (Thames & Hudson, London, 1998)

Buckberrough, Sherry, A., 'Simultaneity in Painting, Poetry and Pochoir', *Sonia Delaunay: A Retrospective* (intro. R. Buck; exh. cat., Albright Knox Art Gallery, Buffalo, New York, USA, 1980)

Cawthorne, Nigel, *The New Look: The Dior Revolution* (Hamlyn, London, 1996)

Celant, Germano (ed.), *Art/Fashion* (exh. cat. Looking at Fashion, Biennale di Firenze: Skira, Florence, 21 September 1996 — 12 January 1997)

Derycke, Luc, & van de Veire, Sandra (eds), *Belgian Fashion Design* (Ludion, Ghent — Amsterdam, 1997)

Frankel, Susannah, 'Like It or Lump It', *Guardian*, 1 March 1997

Frankel, Susannah, *Visionaries, Interviews with Fashion Designers* (V&A, London, 2001)

Haye, Amy de la, & Wilson, Elizabeth (eds), *Defining Dress: Dress as Object, Meaning and Identity* (Manchester U. Press, Manchester & New York, 1999)

Hayward Gallery, London, *Addressing the Century: 100 Years of Art and Fashion* (exh. cat., 1998)

Holborn, Mark, *Issey Miyake* (Taschen, Tokyo, Japan)

Hollander, Anne, *Seeing through Clothes* (Viking, New York, 1978)

Kazuko Sato, 'Issey Miyake Freedom Clothes', *Domus*, 798, November 1997, pp.98–107

Koda, H., Martin, R., and Sinderbrand, L., *Three Women: Rei Kawakubo, Claire McCardell and Madeleine Vionnet* (exh. cat., Fashion Institute of Technology, New York, 1987)

Mendes, Valerie, *Black in Fashion* (V&A, London, 1999)

Mendes, Valerie, & Haye, Amy de la, *Twentieth-century Fashion* (Thames & Hudson, London, 1999)

Miyake, Issey, *East Meets West* (Heibonsha, Japan, 1978)

Miyake, Issey, with Penn, Irving, *Issey Miyake with Photographs by Irving Penn* (New York Graphic Society, USA, 1988)

Steele, Valerie, *Fifty Years of Fashion: New Look to Now* (Yale U. Press, New Haven & London, 1997)

Sudjic, Deyan, *Rei Kawakubo and Comme des Garçons* (Fourth Estate, London, 1990)

Tucker, Andrew, *The London Fashion Book* (Thames & Hudson, London; Rizzoli, New York: 1998)

Wilcox, Claire, and Mendes, Valerie, *Modern Fashion in Detail* (V&A, London, 1998)

Picture Captions & Credit Lines

Looking Forward: Judith Clark

Left to Right

Top row: Maison Martin Margiela, Spring/Summer 1999 (photo: Roberto Tecchio); Henry van de Velde, 1902 (photo: V&A)
Second row: Marcel Duchamp, *Nude Descending a Staircase, No.2*, 1912 (© Succession Marcel Duchamp/ADAGP, Paris, and DACS, London, 2001); John Galliano, Autumn/Winter 1998–99 (photo: Roberto Tecchio)
Third row: Ernesto Thayaht, *Tuta* (photo: V&A); Helmut Lang, Autumn/Winter 2000 (photo: Roberto Tecchio)
Fourth row: Madeleine Vionnet, Advertisement Drawing in *Gazette du Bon Ton*, 1922 (Ernesto Thayaht, photo: V&A); Madeleine Vionnet, Advertisement Drawing in *Gazette du Bon Ton*, 1922 (Ernesto Thayaht, photo: V&A); Madeleine Vionnet, Advertisement Drawing in *Gazette du Bon Ton*, 1922 (Ernesto Thayaht, photo: V&A); Madeleine Vionnet, Advertisement Drawing in *Gazette du Bon Ton*, 1923 (Ernesto Thayaht, photo: V&A)
Bottom row: Giacomo Balla, *Velocity of Cars and Light*, 1913 (© DACS 2001)

Radical Traditionalists: Susannah Frankel

Left to Right

Top row: Maison Martin Margiela Spring/Summer 2000 (photo: Chris Moore); Vivienne Westwood, Storm in a Tea Cup, Autumn/Winter 1996 (photo: Chris Moore)
Second row: Issey Miyake, Constructible Cloth, 1970 (photo: Kishin Shinoyana); Comme des Garçons, Autumn/Winter 2000 (photo: Chris Moore)
Third row: Yohji Yamamoto, Autumn/Winter 1998–99 (photo: Monica Feudi); Azzedine Alaïa, 1985 (photo: V&A, T.374-1985); Azzedine Alaïa, 1985 (photo: V&A, T.376-1985)
Bottom row: Jean Paul Gaultier, Autumn/Winter 2000–01 (photo: Chris Moore); Jean Paul Gaultier, Autumn/Winter 1999 (photo: Chris Moore)

'A Dress is No Longer a Little, Flat Closed Thing': Amy de la Haye

Left to Right

Top row: Issey Miyake, Spring/Summer 1977, *Paradise Lost* print designed by Tadanori Yokoo (photo: Noriaki Yokosuka); Comme des Garçons, Direct mailing cards, Spring/Summer 1994 (photo: Cindy Sherman); Comme des Garçons, 1982 (photo: V&A, T.167-1985)
Second row: Yohji Yamamoto, Autumn/Winter 1986–87 (photo: Nick Knight); Issey Miyake, A-POC, Making Things exhibition at the ACE Gallery, New York, Nov. 1999 (photo: Yasuki Yoshinaga)
Third row: Comme des Garçons, Spring/Summer 1997 (photo: J. François Jose); Comme des Garçons, Spring/Summer 1997 (photo: J. François Jose); Issey Miyake, A-POC 2000 (photo: Friedemann Hauss)
Fourth row: Yohji Yamamoto, Autumn/Winter 1988–89 (art direction: Marc Ascoli; photo: Nick Knight); Junya Watanabe Comme des Garçons, Autumn/Winter 2000–01 (photo: J. François Jose)
Fifth row: Comme des Garçons, Direct Mailing cards, Spring/Summer 1994 (photo: Cindy Sherman); Junya Watanabe Comme des Garçons, Autumn/Winter 2000–01 (photo: J. François Jose)
Bottom row: Issey Miyake, Pleats Please Guest Artists Series, Making Things exhibition at the Fondation Cartier pour L'Art Contemporain, Paris, Oct. 1998 (photo: Yasuki Yoshinaga)

Imagining Fashion: Alistair O'Neill

Left to Right

Top row: Busby Berkeley scene from William Dieterle's *Fashions of 1934*, 1934 (Ronald Grant Archive); Gilbert & George, *The Singing Sculpture*, 1991 (photo: Jon & Anne Abbot; from C. Ratcliff and R. Rosenblum, *Gilbert & George: The Singing Sculpture,* Anthony McCall, New York/Thames & Hudson, 1993)
Second row: Cindy Sherman, *Untitled*, 1979 (courtesy Cindy Sherman and Metro Pictures); Prada advertisement, Spring/Summer 2000 (photo: Robert Wyatt; stylist: Lucy Ewing)
Third row: Prada Interior, *0 Tix 9,* 1998 (photo: Andreas Gursky; courtesy Victoria Miro Gallery, London); Helmut Lang advertisement, Autumn/Winter 2000–01 (photo: Stephen Wong)
Fourth row: Viktor & Rolf, Spring/Summer 2001 (photo: Cavan Pawson, courtesy of *Evening Standard*); Helmut Lang advertisement, Autumn/Winter 1998–99 with 'Man in Polyester Suit 1980' (photo: Robert Mapplethorpe, © The Estate of Robert Mapplethorpe)
Fifth row: The Master of Ceremonies (Anton Walbrook) from Max Ophuls's *La Ronde*, 1950 (Ronald Grant Archive); Maison Martin Margiela, Autumn/Winter 1998–99, marionette presentation by Jane How (photo: Marina Faust, Paris); Maison Martin Margiela, Autumn/Winter 1998–99, marionette presentation by Jane How (photo: Anders Edström)
Bottom row: Prada advertisement, Spring/Summer 2000 (photo: Robert Wyatt; stylist: Lucy Ewing)

'Style in Revolt': Valerie Steele

Left to Right
Top row: Vivienne Westwood, Portrait, Autumn/Winter 1990 (photo: Niall McInerney); Vivienne Westwood, Seditionaries, 1977 (model: Debbie Juvenile, photo: Vivienne Westwood archive); Vivienne Westwood, Dressing Up, Autumn/Winter 1991 (photo: Niall McInerney)
Second row: John Galliano, 1988 (photo: V&A, T.389-1988); Alexander McQueen, Spring/Summer 2001 (photo: Chris Moore); Alexander McQueen, Autumn/Winter 1998 (photo: Robert Fairer)
Third row: Alexander McQueen, Spring/Summer 2000 (photo: Chris Moore); Hussein Chalayan, Between, Spring/Summer 1998 (photo: Chris Moore); Hussein Chalayan, Panoramic, Autumn/Winter 1998 (photo: Chris Moore)
Bottom row: Hussein Chalayan, Echoform, Autumn/Winter 1999 (photo: Chris Moore)

The Designers

p.56: *i-D*, Gallery Issue, 208, April 2001
p.64: Interview by Susannah Frankel with Hussein Chalayan, *The Independent Fashion Magazine*, Spring/Summer 2000
p.72: Rei Kawakubo to Claire Wilcox, 2001
p.73: Comme des Garçons, Spring/Summer 2001, Photo: Yoshiko Seino
p.74: Comme des Garçons, Inspirational Imagery, Spring/Summer 2001, Photo: Yoshiko Seino
p.75: Comme des Garçons, Spring/Summer 2001, Photo: Yoshiko Seino
p.76: Comme des Garçons, Spring/Summer 2001, Photo: Yoshiko Seino
p.77: Comme des Garçons, Inspirational Imagery, Spring/Summer 2001, Photo: Yoshiko Seino
p.78: Comme des Garçons, Spring/Summer 2001, Photo: Yoshiko Seino
p.79: Comme des Garçons, Inspirational Imagery, Spring/Summer 2001, Photo: Yoshiko Seino
p.80: *Self Service*, 13, Autumn/Winter 2000
p.96: *TALK*, March 2001
p.104: Susannah Frankel, *Visionaries, Interviews with Fashion Designers* (V&A, London, 2001)
pp.105–111: All images first published in *The Fashion*, No. 02, S/S 2001
p.112: Susannah Frankel, *Visionaries, Interviews with Fashion Designers* (V&A, London, 2001)
pp.116–17: All images represented here were first published in *The Independent Magazine*, 14 April 1999
p.120: *Scene* Magazine, June 1999
p.121: Junya Watanabe Comme des Garçons, Inspirational Object, Spring/Summer 2000
p.122: Junya Watanabe Comme des Garçons, Spring/Summer 2001
p.123: Junya Watanabe Comme des Garçons, Inspirational Object, Spring/Summer 1999
p.124: Junya Watanabe Comme des Garçons, Autumn/Winter 2000–01
p.125: Junya Watanabe Comme des Garçons, Inspirational Object, Spring/Summer 1996
p.126: Junya Watanabe Comme des Garçons, Autumn/Winter 1998–99
p.127: Junya Watanabe Comme des Garçons, Inspirational Object, Autumn/Winter 2001–02
p.128: Vivienne Westwood to Claire Wilcox, 2001
p.136: Yohji Yamamoto to Claire Wilcox, 2001